THOMAS MERTON'S
AMERICAN PROPHECY

❖

(Courtesy Gethsemani Abbey Archives)

Thomas Merton's American Prophecy

Robert Inchausti

STATE UNIVERSITY OF NEW YORK PRESS

Production by Ruth Fisher
Marketing by Anne M. Valentine

Published by
State University of New York Press, Albany

For information, address the State University of New York Press,
State University Plaza, Albany, NY 12246

Library of Congress Cataloging-in-Publication Data

Inchausti, Robert, 1952–
    Thomas Merton's American prophecy / Robert Inchausti.
        p.   cm.
    Includes bibliographical references and index.
    ISBN 0–7914–3635–7 (hc : alk. paper). — ISBN 0–7914–3636–5
(pb : alk. paper)
    1. Merton. Thomas, 1915–1968.   2. Trappists—United States—
Biography.   3. Monks—United States—Biography.   I. Title.
BX4705.M542I53   1998
271'.12502—dc21
[B]   97–19155
                                                                      CIP

10   9   8   7   6   5   4   3   2   1

To Linda, Monica, and Nicholas,
for standing over me and inviting me
with unutterable sweetness
to be awake and to live.

Strange that the individual is the only power that is left. And though his power is zero, zero has great power when one understands it and knows where to place it.

—Thomas Merton, in a letter to Henry Miller

Contents

Acknowledgments

This book has been a voyage of discovery for me, and I owe a debt of gratitude to all those who have taken me further into the life and thought of Thomas Merton. Particular thanks go to the Merton scholars I met at the International Thomas Merton Society Convention in Colorado Springs, Colorado, in 1993: William H. Shannon, Robert E. Daggy, Brother Patrick Hart, A. M. Allchin, Ron Sietz, Jeff Kiernan, Mary Murray, Thomas Del Prete, Kenneth M. Voiles, Jeannete Cantrell, and the many others whose talks I attended but did not have the pleasure of meeting personally.

I also owe a particular debt to Czeslaw Milosz for taking the time to discuss his friendship with Thomas Merton and to Professors Victor Comerchero, Robert Garlitz, Harvey Kaye, and Elliot Gorn, for their telling criticisms of earlier drafts of this manuscript.

Thanks also go to my friends Gary Cooper, Leonard Larson, Alan Howell, Mark Roberts, Jim Cushing, Wayne C. Booth, Mike Wenzl, Mary Giles, Paula Huston, Hunter Lillis, Linda Halisky, Jim Howland, Judy Saltzman, Catherine Lucas, Ken Brown, George Diestel, Maurice Friedman, Peter Turner, John Dobby Boe, and Tom King who—although they might not have always known it—have served as boon companions for me along Merton's dark path.

I also owe a debt of gratitude to my student assistants at Cal Poly: James K. West, Jennifer Hertz, David Welch, and Warren Oberman, whose energy and idealism served as a constant inspiration.

The CUSHWA Center for the Study of American Catholicism provided me with a grant to visit the Hesburgh Library at Notre Dame to study archives on the Catholic Peace Fellowship. Particular thanks go to Kevin Cawley, associate archivist and Charlotte Ames, reference librarian, for their help and professionalism.

Thanks also go to David D. Cooper for his encouragement during the early stages of this project, Rosemary Ruether, Annie Dillard, Guy Davenport, and Wendell Berry for their generous replies to my queries, and to Paul Zingg and The School of Liberal Arts at Cal Poly for granting me a summer stipend to complete this work. Special thanks also go to Janice Stone Rose and Zoe Brazil from the interlibrary loan department at Kennedy Library at Cal Poly whose efforts made this book possible.

INTRODUCTION

Thomas Merton was a man of many contradictions: a monk who advocated nonviolent revolution, a poet who believed silence was the ultimate eloquence, a social critic who distrusted sociological categories, and a world-famous hermit. These riddles do not untie themselves easily. In fact, they do not untie themselves at all but rather point toward a prophetic religious sensibility in which they merge as complementary aspects of a single, unified vision. This vision can, perhaps, best be understood in the light of Søren Kierkegaard's distinction between the genius and the apostle.

The genius, according to Kierkegaard, has "only an immanent teleology," while the apostle is "absolutely, paradoxically, teleologically placed."[1] Genius, in other words, is the fulfillment of a human potentiality. It expresses itself in works that are ends in themselves—masterpieces. And those masterpieces define what it means to be human. But apostles are not geniuses. They exist in a paradoxical relationship to the human enterprise. They are, if you will, contradictions to humanity as an end in itself. Apostles point beyond achievement, beyond history, beyond even life itself, to some as yet unimagined end. They are absolute dissidents and metaphysical rebels whose primary contribution to everyday life is to overcome its falsity and limitations by drowning them in the light of a higher truth.

Thomas Merton was an apostle, not a genius. He did not write great poetry or masterpieces of theology. He exposed the half-truths accepted by his countrymen, his church, and the world at large. He preferred questions to answers, ineffable experience to articulated doctrine, the via negativa to positivist social science. He never intended his ideas to be absorbed into society in the form of new laws, regulations, organizations, or schools of prayer. His *telos* was always elsewhere, and his audience never merely human.

Attempts have been made to define the principles Merton served. Archbishop Jean Jadot saw him as somebody who had intuitions, feelings, and the ability to see in what direction to go during a very troubled era. "He was," Jadot said, "a kind of prophet. And I think he will be remembered in the history of spirituality as a man who—I wouldn't say opened *new* ways— he opened old ways we had forgotten. He had the ability to talk in new terms about things or attitudes or values that were common one thousand or fifteen hundred years ago."[2]

W. H. Ferry, Merton's friend and one of the founders of the The Center for the Study of Democratic Institutions in Santa Barbara, California, saw him in more political terms: "The picture of Tom that many people have is one of a monk who wrote marvelously affecting, marvelously instructive books of solemn and profound religious importance. I didn't see very much of that. I saw the other side. I saw a concerned citizen. A beer-drinking good fellow out taking pictures of barns and cemeteries and roots and things like that. A man who liked to walk in the woods and talk. A man who was furious with the way the world was going and couldn't wait to tell people of his fury."[3]

Neither of these remarks, however telling, do justice to the full extent of Merton's radicalism. Merton himself could find appropriate analogies for what he was attempting to accomplish only in the Old Testament oracles, Zen Koans, commentaries of the Mystics, myths of the Oaxaca Indians, novels of William Faulkner, essays of Albert Camus, and the poems of Rainer Maria Rilke. Virtually all the people Merton ever wrote about or admired were "apostles" in Kierkegaard's sense of the term: Meister Eckhart, William Blake, Chuang Tzu, Gandhi, Franz Jaggarstatter (the working man who was beheaded for refusing national service under Hitler), Alfred Delp (the Jesuit martyr executed by the Nazis in 1945), Boris Pasternak, Dietrich Bonhoeffer, Ishi, D. T. Suzuki, Kitaro Nishida, Saint Theresa, and Saint John of the Cross.

What is common to each of these figures is that they assumed the authority of an undefinable, exterior *telos* that brought them into conflict with the prevailing pieties of their age. Each of them followed their conscience to assert a moral and intellectual sovereignty beyond anything granted them by the world at large, and by so doing invented the very values by which they themselves were to be interpreted and understood. Their testimonies, like Merton's, often went unheeded, lost beneath historical trends and fashions only to reemerge generations later as the most accurate interpretations of the peculiar outrages of their times.

Those who are engaged by Merton's work—and he has a large if highly individualistic following—are not taken by his doctrines so much as by his candor, by his ability to speak directly to their solitude through a rigorous examination of his own. His writings close the gap between the readers' exterior, historical lives and their undetermined, interior freedom—between their worldly selves tied to illusory dreams and ambitions and the new Adam they are all in the process of becoming. As a result, Merton's writing succeeds—not when it persuades readers to change their ideas, but when the tension between who those readers really *are* and who they profess to be comes to rest in a shared existential recognition. When this happens, the reader's false self stands defeated, and he or she is left with a strange sense of having been both "found out" and "set free"—both morally convicted and spiritually redeemed.

Merton described his goals as a writer this way: "It is not as an author that I would speak to you, not as a story-teller, not as a philosopher, not as a friend only: I seek to speak to you, in some way, as your own self. Who can tell what this may mean? I myself do not know. But if you listen, things will be said that are perhaps not written in this book. And this will be due not to me, but to One who lives and speaks in both!"[4]

In 1993 I came to understand Merton's unique appeal when I attended the convention of the International Thomas Merton Society in Colorado Springs, Colorado. The meeting had its share of academics interested in Merton scholarship, but there were also a number of Zen Buddhists from Japan, political dissidents from China, Beat poets from San Francisco and New

York, Maryknoll nuns from Asia and Latin America, not to mention an eclectic collection of priests, housewives, school teachers, and lay religious from around the world. There was even a dance therapist from Seattle and a millionaire businessman on a metaphysical journey. All of these people saw Merton as the living, breathing embodiment of their own religious aspirations. His life and work, indeed his very voice and person, gave expression to their own sense of themselves as spiritual beings trapped within a twentieth-century secular Diaspora.

Merton inspires because he remained faithful to who he was and to all that he knew in times of great social upheaval. Whatever the issue, he brought the full measure of his wisdom to bear on the matters at hand. The clash of various religious traditions that has led so many to embrace odd, new bohemian syntheses became for him a productive avenue of thought. His scholastic training, united with his existential sensibility acquired as a man come of age in the tumultuous thirties, allowed him to combine the desert spirituality of the Church Fathers with the cosmopolitan concerns of the New York Intellectuals to formulate one of the most eloquent defenses of individual autonomy of the entire postwar period.

What follows is a evaluation of Thomas Merton's place in American intellectual history. No attempt has been made to compete with the larger biographies or specialized studies. The emphasis here is entirely upon his unique defense of the individual conscience and the role that defense plays—or should play—in contemporary American life. To do this, I will follow the evolution of his thought from his studies with Mark Van Doren at Columbia in the thirties, through his conversations with Czeslaw Milosz in the late fifties, all the way up to his journey to the East in 1968. By retracing his steps, I hope to demonstrate that Merton was the quintessential American outsider who defined himself in opposition to the world around him and then discovered in the alternative values with which he opposed the world a way back into dialogue with it and compassion for it.

Thomas Merton was not a spokesman for any particular group, cause, or movement, but a critic of any and all manifestations of bad faith: the harbinger of a still yet to be realized personalist counterculture. In the sixties his unique contemplative social criticism comprised the most forthright and compelling Orthodox alternative to the profound critiques of postindustrial society offered by the New Left. He was, is, and remains the embodied antithesis of the postmodern: Jack Kerouac's monastic older brother; Norman Mailer's Golden Shadow; and the as yet unacknowledged precursor, alternative, and heir to Norman O. Brown's defense of mystery in the life of the mind.

But in order to understand the significance of this description and the full meaning of Thomas Merton's American Prophecy, we must begin where he began, in the South of France, just before the start of World War I.

CHAPTER ONE

EARLY LIFE

Thomas Merton spent the first twenty years of life tossed about in a sea of conflicting influences. He was born in Prades, France, in 1915, just a few hundred miles away from the killing fields of World War I and grew up in the shadows of international conflict, domestic tragedy, and radical social instability. His parents were both artists who had met in 1911 while studying at the Academy of Percyval Tudor-Hart in Paris. His father, Owen Merton, a devotee of Cézanne, was born in New Zealand, and his mother, Ruth Calvert Jenkins, a student of dance and interior design, was born in New York.

Yet despite his father's fascination with Cubism and his mother's interest in the emerging new design movement, neither of them ever came into contact with any of the giants of Parisian modernism. Merton described his parents as "possessing the integrity of artists—an integrity that lifted them above the level of the world without delivering them from it."[1] They were, to his mind, tragic figures who, like many of their generation, sought in art what they could not find in life: occasions and objects worthy of adoration.

Before the armies began to scatter bodies and shells over the French countryside, Merton's family moved to Long Island to be closer to his mother's parents. It was there that his only brother John Paul was born in 1918, and there that his mother died of stomach cancer three years later.

Merton was only six years old at the time of his mother's death, and the loss haunted him for the rest of his life. Not only did the loss inflict emotional turmoil and inconsolable loneliness upon him, it left him to be raised by an itinerant father who spent a great deal of time traveling the world trying to get his painting career off the ground. Consequently, as a child Merton never really had a home. He was constantly being shuttled back and forth from wherever his father happened to be living to his grandparents' home on Long Island.

This arrangement, however, did have its advantages. Besides providing Merton with an international education and fluency in two languages, it also allowed him to develop an intimate relationship with his grandfather, Samuel (Pop) Jenkins. In contrast to his father, Pop was an American self-made man who had started out as a newspaper boy and through sheer hard work had become a successful sheet-music salesman. "Pop" invented a picture book using stills from movies to tell stories, and it made him a small fortune—part of which eventually paid for Merton's education.

In 1925, when Merton was ten years old, he moved back to France with his father and enrolled in the Lycee Ingres at Montauban. Merton's younger Brother, John Paul, stayed behind with the Jenkins's. Although John Paul visited Merton during the summers, the absence and the distance hurt their relationship. Merton felt an older brother's sense of responsibility for this loss of connection, along with an older brother's feelings of utter helplessness at ever being able to heal it.

Years later, when John Paul died in World War II, Merton expressed his anguish in one of the most moving poems he ever composed. But in 1925, he took the separation stoically, and though he felt isolated and alone at the Lycee, he was inspired by French delicacy, grace, intelligence, and taste—things he hadn't really known in Pop's house where the emphasis had been upon movie stars, success, and the family's new affluence.

It didn't take the young Merton long, however, to notice the cynicism of the boys at the Lycee. They seemed, he tells us in his autobiography, bent upon "transforming their intelligence into sophistry; and their dignity and refinement into petty vanity and theatrical self-display."[2] Of course, he mentions all this in retrospect. A boy of ten, even one as precocious as he, could not have been able to formulate such criticism consciously. Yet it is clear that he felt the sting of the pseudo-sophistication of the French bourgeoisie at a very tender age, and it left its mark. It drove him into a literary underground of sorts populated by friends in the lower grades who had taken it upon themselves to compose long and complicated epic adventure novels in the tradition of Jules Verne. These kids, Merton tells us, "still had ideals and ambitions," and so he joined them, finding in writing an escape from the pressures and pretensions of the world around him.

Three years later, Merton's father moved to England to be closer to the London art scene, and Merton found himself enrolled in Ripley Court School in Surrey. The understated expectation for excellence in the British public schools suited him far more than the arrogance of Mountauban, and he blossomed as a student. He graduated to Oakham Public School a year later and stayed there until his admission to Cambridge University in the fall of 1933.

It somehow seems fitting that Merton was part of the generation who came of age in England between the two great wars. The British Empire may have been outwardly declining, but inwardly it was gathering strength for its final stand against the emerging totalitarian plague. To enter manhood at such a time and place was to be confronted by great issues and much social strife, and yet to know in one's bones that nonchalant heroic resolve was the sine qua non of adult life.

Two years after entering Oakham, Merton's father died of a brain tumor leaving him virtually alone in the world. Grandfather Jenkins and John Paul were an ocean away. And although they still sometimes visited him during the summers and Pop continued to provide him with financial assistance, Merton began to lose his sense of purpose and direction. He did well enough as a student to be admitted into Cambridge, but he was beginning to acquire a reputation as a rebel and self-styled outsider. He began to smoke a pipe, wear turtleneck sweaters, and listen to hot jazz recordings rather than to the swing records the other students liked.[3] And although he talked about a career in the diplomatic corps, his actual aspirations were far less admirable.

"I was not really content at Oakham at all," he later wrote, "but only wanted to get my scholarship to Cambridge and get away. And what I would do then, was go looking for a girl and . . . happiness. And the way to find a fine girl was to go where the fine girls were: and as I knew from movies and novels, the really pretty girls, the gay and witty graceful ones who dressed well and were really beautiful, were in theaters and nightclubs and big dances. And at Clubs and Hotels on the Rivera, and in cities and everywhere where life was itself fine and gay and beautiful and full of light and richness and gaiety. Because fine things all go together, and if I were there where beautiful things like newly decorated modernist bars, and places where there was good music, there I would find beautiful women."[4]

Merton entered Clare College, Cambridge, in the fall, but his first and only year there was an unmitigated disaster. Although the facts are sketchy, it seems that among his many indiscretions that year, he fathered a child out of wedlock, participated as the victim in a mock crucifixion at a drunken fraternity party, lost a goodly portion of his academic scholarship, and generally made a mess of his young life.

He retreated to New York and entered Columbia University in January 1935. It was not an auspicious return. When Merton got back to the United States, freed from his European entanglements, he was morally lost. Like many of the college students of his era, his primary enthusiasms were avant-garde literature, sex, alcohol, and notoriety. He looked to radical politics for direction, and during his first year at Columbia he joined the Communist Party, protesting the Italian invasion of Ethiopia, taking the "Oxford Pledge" and participating in rallies, shouting such slogans as "Books, not Battleships! No more War!" He even had his own party name: "Frank Swift."[5]

But Merton was not a very dedicated communist. He attended only one meeting, which he found insufferably boring. Later he admitted that his interest in politics had less to do with any sense of social responsibility than with his own personal search for meaning. "The thing that made Communism seem so plausible to me, was my own lack of logic which failed to distinguish between the reality of the evils which Communism was trying to overcome and the validity of its diagnosis and chosen cure. For there can be no doubt that modern society is in a terrible condition, and that its wars and depressions and its slums and all its other evils are principally the fruits of an unjust social system, a system that must be reformed and purified or else replaced. However, if you are wrong does that make me right? If you are bad, does that prove that I am good?"[6]

This is a telling repudiation because it points to Merton's early recognition of a basic psychological flaw in vulgar appropriations of Marx and Freud. There is a vast difference between exposing a fraud and defending a value. The ideas of Marx had appealed to Merton precisely because they served his youthful need for self-justification. Marxism offered a way to repudiate an obviously flawed social order without having to acknowledge any particular moral flaws in himself, and so it played into his own rootless egotism by exempting him from any rigorous examination of conscience.

Fortunately there were several critics of modern culture at Columbia who tempered Merton's facile political theorizing and exposed the self-serving premises behind his pseudo-revolt. Most notable among these were Joseph Wood Krutch, Lionel Trilling, Jacques Barzun, and Mark Van Doren. Van Doren had a particularly powerful impact upon Merton. His love of literature as a way of making sense of the world, as a virtue of the practical intellect and not simply a vague spilling of emotions, inspired Merton to direct his considerable intellectual energies toward a literary career and unknowingly prepared the way for Merton's eventual religious conversion.

Van Doren, Merton observed, looked for the quiddities of things, and sought being and substance under the cover of accident and appearance. This protoscholasticism served as a counterpoint to Merton's own fascination with dialectics. "It was a very good thing that I ran into someone like Mark Van Doren at that particular time because in my new reverence for Communism, I was in danger of docilely accepting any kind of stupidity, provided I thought it was something that paved the way to the Elysian fields of classless society."[7]

Merton quickly became disillusioned with what he called "the radical mystique," but he never lost his conviction that extreme measures were needed to meet the crises of the age. He had just become convinced that those measures had to be personal and symbolic ones. The so-called activists were actually making things worse by accentuating the very features of modernity most in need of reform: its penchant for shrill, reductive explanations of complex social phenomena and its fascination with change for change's sake.

It is difficult to over estimate the impact Columbia had on Merton. He began to read in a new, more Emersonian fashion, directly linking books to life. Van Doren had taught him that by age eighteen or nineteen one finally has had enough experiences to read literature profitably.[8] Merton was being invited to shed the veneer of his European sophistication and become an "American Scholar"—someone who "resisted the vulgar prosperity that retrogrades ever to barbarism, by preserving and communicating heroic sentiments, noble biographies, melodious verse, and the conclusions of history."[9]

Inspired, Merton threw himself into his writing and into his studies—becoming the editor of the yearbook, a member of all the literary clubs, an athlete on the track team, and a brother of the Alpha Delta Phi fraternity. As he entered his senior year at Columbia in 1937, although he didn't know it at the time, both he and the world were on the verge of profound transformations.

The thirties had been a time when things seemed to dart back and forth in a hundred different directions. Democratic societies came under fire for lack of resolve, and the flaws of Capitalism were exposed by its stark failures of distribution. The rise of the industrial state, rather than leading to an era of abundance, seemed to have actually disenfranchised the common man, creating unemployment and making possible terrible new forms of warfare. The decade had opened with the stock market crash, the Great Depression, Hitler's ascension to the chancellorship of Germany. And it was ending with the Nazis invading Poland.

Thomas Merton was becoming a "man thinking" at the very moment that European culture was reaching its philosophical nadir. Outside forces were now dictating the terms of individual existence to a degree hitherto unimaginable, and the relationship between ends and means, between life and production, indeed, between subject and object, were rapidly becoming inverted and debased. If Hegel was right, and the life of the mind only attains its truth when discovering itself in absolute desolation, then Merton could not have picked a better time to embark upon his journey of self-discovery.

CHAPTER TWO

CONVERSION

In February 1937, while preparing for a French literature class, Merton stumbled upon Etienne Gilson's book *The Spirit of Medieval Philosophy*. There he discovered for the first time in his life an intellectually respectable notion of God. God was not *a* Being; God was Being *itself*. If this was true, if this was the way religious thinkers understood the concept, then all those sophomoric debates about God's existence couched in the narrow, epistemological terms of Enlightenment skepticism were simply beside the point. One could read Medieval theology as food for self-making without abandoning logic, science, or common sense.

This was a stunning revelation for Merton, and it opened him up to whole new ways of thinking about religion and about the past. He began to explore Christian theology as a viable alternative to the materialist and naturalist philosophies of his day. He could see now why faith in God was for so many "a cogent necessity."[1] It needn't be a crutch or an evasion; it could serve as a creative trope that gave one access to mysteries of existence accessible in no other way. God as Being was a more radical a priori than either the Cartesian cogito or Nietzschean nihilism.

Merton's friend, the poet Robert Lax,[2] seeing the liberating effect Gilson's book had on Merton, suggested that he read Aldous Huxley's *Ends and Means*—a consideration of politics and social issues from a mystical point of view. Huxley argued that social reform was predicated upon the reeducation of the individual will and that ascetic practices held the key, not only to personal happiness, but to social justice. Merton was so impressed with the book that he published a review of it, and then wrote directly to Huxley himself.[3] He even chased down the Asian religious texts mentioned in the footnotes.

After graduating in June 1938, Merton entered the Master's program at Columbia in English. A Hindu monk Brachmachari, who was teaching there at the time, encouraged him to read the Christian contemplatives before dabbling in the wisdom of the East, specifically suggesting Augustine's *Confessions* and Thomas á Kempis's *Imitation of Christ*. Merton read these books immediately and found them to be bold assaults upon the complacencies of his own age. He began to go to mass and practice the rudiments of contemplative prayer. He even changed his thesis topic from an analysis of the eighteenth-century satirical novel *The Spiritual Quixote* by Richard Graves, to a study of William Blake.

It was a fortuitous decision, for in the course of his research he ran into Jacques Maritain's *Art and Scholasticism*. This book, Merton tells us, "untied all the knots in the problem" he had set to solve in his thesis, "the problem of reconciling art with nature in an age of mechanization."[4]

"I had imagined," Merton wrote, "that Blake, like the other Romantics, was glorifying passion, natural energy, for their own sake. Far from it! What he was glorifying was the transfiguration of man's natural love, his natural powers, in the refining fires of mystical experience: and that in itself, implied an arduous and total purification, by faith and love and desire, from all the petty materialistic and commonplace and earthly ideals of his rationalistic friends."[5]

Seen through the eyes of Gilson and Maritain, Blake was not advocating revolution so much as updating and extending the Christian virtues as a way of channeling natural energies toward harmony, perfection, and balance.[6] Naturalism didn't channel these energies; it merely reflected them, and so it failed as a basis for aesthetics or morality. The Medieval theological wager, if one can call it that, offered a way of bringing the longing for beauty and justice back into dialogue with the material cosmos and the fallen world. Merton found this a far more inspiring, not to say pragmatic, way to proceed. Instead of chasing one's epistemological tail in a neverending quest for the trope behind all tropes, the first cause, or the premiseless premise, one simply admitted that Being preceded both existence and essence and as such could not be thought.

At the time he was writing his thesis, Merton was still a long way away from making these ideas his own. He remarks in *The Seven Storey Mountain*: "Oh, how blind and weak and sick I was, although I thought I saw where I was going, and half understood the way! How deluded we sometimes are by the clear notions we get out of books. They make us think that we really understand things of which we have no practical knowledge at all. I remember how learnedly and enthusiastically I could talk for hours about mysticism and experiential knowledge of God, and all the while I was stoking the fires of the argument with Scotch and soda."[7]

Merton mentions Scotch and soda here, not because he was opposed to drinking alcohol. In fact, Merton was a rather enthusiastic beer drinker his entire life. He is merely pointing out the necessity of practicing what you preach. And the more Merton studied Catholicism, the more convinced he became that he had to change his life.

In September 1938, he began formal instruction for admittance into the Catholic Church. By doing this, he was not just following through on the logic of Gilson, Huxley, and Maritain, but was declaring to himself and to the world a radical transformation in his own allegiances and self-conception. He no longer aspired, like Stephen Dedalus and so many other writers of his generation, to forge in the smithy of his soul the uncreated conscience of his race, but rather to reawaken and redeem his own lost completeness.

"We do not have to create a conscience for ourselves," he wrote, "we are born with one, and no matter how much we may ignore it, we cannot silence its insistent demand that we do good and avoid evil. No matter how much we may deny our freedom and our moral responsibility, our intellectual soul cries out for a morality and a spiritual freedom without which it knows it cannot be happy."[8]

Merton's conversion was both an act of self-affirmation and an act of contrition. It was his way of repudiating his own youthful megalomania. But it was also his way of ascending to the spiritual heights. Merton had always wanted to be a great man, but he had also always wanted to live truly. In Catholicism he found a way to do both. He would lose himself in order to find himself. Conversion was a beautiful, if perhaps a bit convenient, antidote for overcoming the unhappy, alienated, self-seeking modern he had become without capitulating to the slave morality of a conventional existence.

At this time in his life, I think it would be fair to say that Merton had seen through his false self[9] but had not yet attained to the contemplative alternative. He knew that he was called to a life of service, he just wasn't sure to what particular form of service he was actually called. In order to find out, he began to factor into each and every one of his experiences an eschatological perspective. That is to say, he began to consider things from the point of view of eternity.

He conceived of the idea of joining a monastery during a conversation with Robert Lax, as they were walking down Sixth Avenue in New York in the spring of 1939. As Merton tells the story, Lax had just asked him what he wanted to be. Merton knew he couldn't say he wanted to be "the well-known writer of all those book reviews in the back pages of the *Times Book Review*," or Thomas Merton the assistant instructor of Freshman English at the New Life Social Institute for Progress and Culture, so he put the thing on the spiritual plane, where he knew it belonged and said: "I don't know; I guess what I want is to be a good Catholic."[10]

Lax challenged him. "What do you mean, you want to be a good Catholic? What you should say is that you want to be a saint."

When Merton asked him how he could become a saint, Lax replied, "By wanting to."

"I can't be a saint," Merton remembers saying, "I can't be a saint." And his mind, Merton tells us, darkened with "a confusion of realities and unrealities: the knowledge of his own sins, and the false humility which makes people say that they cannot do the things they must."[11]

This account is one of the most celebrated and yet misunderstood passages in *The Seven Storey Mountain*. Merton's point is not that by desiring to become a saint, anyone can become one—that idea belonged to Lax (and before him to St. Thomas Aquinas). Merton's point was more circumspect and more modern: What keeps us from *wanting* to become saints is our mistaken belief that we know what a saint is. Merton's point here—and one of the key themes of his autobiography—is that there is a vast difference between good intentions and purity of intention. Seeking to do the right thing is not as important as seeking to know what the right thing to do is. Willing the good is not sufficient; one must first know what good to will.

At this point in his life Merton was just beginning to consider the possibility that what he thought was good may in fact be evil. As an educated modern man, he had just assumed that what he wanted for himself was what he should have. But Lax's remark had forced upon him the realization that a sincere man is not someone who acts on what he believes, but someone who serves the truth by questioning his own beliefs.[12]

Lax told Merton that America was a country of people who desperately wanted to be kind and pleasant and happy and serve God, but didn't know how because they were surrounded by all kinds of information that bewildered them. They needed "someone capable of telling them of the love of God in a language that did not sound cliché or crazy but resonated with authority and conviction born of sanctity." They needed a homegrown saint.[13]

Merton never forgot that conversation although he feared that he had already forfeited his claim to any "convictions born of sanctity." Still, a few weeks later, after taking a job teaching English at Columbia extension, he purchased a copy of the first volume of the works of St. John of the Cross and began to read "The Counsels to a Religious on How to Reach Perfection." This treatise included admonishments toward resignation, mortification, the practice of virtue, and bodily and spiritual solitude. Merton figured that if he could not be a saint himself, he ought to at least know what one was.

Several months later while sitting on the floor of his apartment, playing records with friends and eating his breakfast, he suddenly decided that he was going to become a priest. "I cannot say what caused it," he later wrote, "it was not a reaction of especially strong disgust at being so tired and so uninterested in this life I was leading, in spite of its futility. It was not the music, not the fall air, for this conviction which had suddenly been planted in me full grown was not the sick and haunting sort of thing that an emotional urge always is. It was not a thing of passion or of fancy. It was a strong and sweet and deep and insistent attraction that suddenly made itself felt, but not as movement of appetite towards any sensible good. It was something in the order of conscience, a new and profound and clear sense that this was what I really ought to do."[14]

Merton applied to the Franciscan Order in the fall of 1939 and was accepted into the novitiate class of August 1940, which meant he had to wait almost a full year before he could be admitted. He took advantage of the time by going through St. Ignatius's Spiritual Exercises and taking Daniel Walsh's class on Medieval Philosophy. He was receiving communion every day now while the war raged in Europe.

On May 21, 1940, he wrote in his journal: "If I don't pretend, like other people to understand the war, I do know this much: that the knowledge of what is going on only makes it seem desperately important to be voluntarily poor, to get rid of all possessions this instant. I am scared, sometimes to own anything, even a name, let alone coin, or shares in oil, the munitions, the airplane factories. I am scared to take a proprietary interest in anything, for fear that my love of what I own may be killing somebody somewhere."[15]

These remarks are really less interesting as an anticipation of Merton's later qualified pacifism than they are symptomatic of his radical honesty. He is willing to admit that the war baffles him and own up to the truth, even if that truth is only the negative knowledge that the war had implicated us all in a great folly.

But the long delay in his admittance to the Franciscans began to fray his emotions and weaken his confidence in himself. During Easter break in 1940, he visited Cuba, making a pilgrimage to the shrine of Our Lady of Cobre. There he prayed to the Virgin that he be made a priest—*if that was God's will*. In June he visited his brother in New York, who had just flunked out of Cornell, and then spent the rest of the summer with his friends Robert Lax and Edward Rice writing novels.

By July Merton was having serious misgivings about his worthiness to join the Franciscans. Giving in to an attack of the scruples, he went to New York in August and confessed his Cambridge sins to Father Edmund. Father Edmund told him that it was probably not a good idea for him to enter the novitiate at this time, and the rejection nearly broke Merton's heart. He wept bitterly, but accepted the judgment, taking it as a sign that he did not have a religious vocation. In the fall he went back to St. Bonaventure to teach English composition.

In the long run Merton's failure to be accepted into the Franciscan Order deepened him. He was beginning to realize how serious a calling he had taken on in wanting to become a Priest. When he got back to St. Bonaventure, he immediately embarked upon a program of self-transformation. He gave up smoking, stopped going to movies, and purged his bookshelf of "immoral influences."

Daniel Walsh, sensing the urgency and depth of Merton's religious longings, suggested that he make a retreat to the Abbey of Gethsemani in Trappist Kentucky. Merton made the retreat in April 1941, and he knew immediately he had found his place in the world. He wrote in his journal: "I should tear out all the other pages of this book, and all the other pages of anything else I have ever written, and begin here. This is the center of America. I had wondered what was holding the country together, what has been keeping the universe from cracking to pieces and falling apart. This is the only real city in America—and it is by itself in the wilderness. It is an axle around which the whole country blindly turns, and knows nothing about it. Gethsemani holds the country together the way the underlying substrata of natural faith that goes with our whole being and can hardly be separated from it, keeps living on in a man who has 'lost his faith' who no longer believes in Being and yet himself *is*, in spite of his crazy denial that He Who IS mercifully allowed him to *be*."[16]

That year, in June, Merton began to write an experimental, autobiographical novel based upon his experiences in England before the war. He called it *The Journal of My Escape from the Nazis*. The book contains a telling dialogue between Merton and two uniformed men who see him sitting behind his typewriter in a house bombed during the London blitz. It expresses Merton's growing conviction that whatever his fate as a religious man, somehow he was going to have to write his way out of the chaos that had become his life. He was unsure how he was going to do this or even that such a strategy made any sense, but if his retreat to Gethsemani had taught him anything, it was that there was an order deeper than sense, a holy gestalt, if you will, behind all of our lives.

When the soldiers ask him who he is, he replies: "I am a writer. I write what I see out the window. I am writing about the fear on the faces of the houses. I say as fast as I can, what preoccupation I see in the sick houses of bombarded London, and I write that the houses of bombarded London do not understand their own fear."

The soldiers then ask him if he has written about them and their courage, and Merton answers, "I have written that you folded your arms and frowned at me from under the shadows of your helmets."[17] This, of course, does not satisfy them, and they demand to know who he is and why he confuses fear with courage. Merton replies, "I am still trying to find out: and that is why I write."

When one of the soldiers asks him how writing can possibly help him find out, Merton offers a succinct description of his early sense of vocation: "I will keep putting things down until they become clear. (And if they do not become clear?) I will have a hundred books, full of symbols, full of everything I ever knew or ever saw or ever thought. . . . Some things are too clear to be understood, and what you think is your understanding of them is only a kind of charm, a kind of incantation in your mind concerning that thing. This is not understanding: it is something you remember. So much for definition! We always have to go back and start from the beginning and make over all the definitions for ourselves again."[18]

These passages make it very clear that the young Thomas Merton was concerned not only with his place in the world but with the meaning of war and the rise of totalitarian states. He was trying to move beyond both tragic and epic conceptions of history and of his own personal life to arrive at some as yet unfathomed spiritual point of view. He truly did not understand "the fabulous courage of soldiers and sailors, dying with their minds full of such weird and ugly lumber."[19] But his saving grace, his genius really, was that he refused to pretend he did. He was brave enough and honest enough to rest, even at this early age, even during these crazy times, at the limit of his understanding.

This is, no doubt, why this first book, although a fascinating record of his concerns as a young man, was not published. To paraphrase his editor Robert Giroux: it didn't go anywhere. If it had attempted to define the limits of human intelligibility, that might have been enough to warrant publication. But Merton was too young to know what those limits were. As a result the novel shifts its boundaries too often, moves back and forth unsure as to the exact location of its own point of view or the ultimate destination of its protagonist.

That summer Baroness de Hueck came to Columbia to lecture on her settlement house in Harlem. Merton had worked there as a volunteer, and after hearing her speak decided to take a permanent job in Harlem starting the following January. In the meantime he continued his daily regimen of forty-five minutes of mental prayer and began to read the autobiography of St. Therese of Lisieux.[20]

St. Therese was an important discovery for Merton because part of his motivation for agreeing to work in Harlem came from lingering middle-class guilt. He wanted to cleanse himself of the bookish artificiality of his protected existence and immerse himself in real life, real work, and real sacrifice. St. Therese showed him that there were other ways to do this than taking on a career as a social worker. She had been able to overcome the smugness of her class to attain real sanctity, and if she could do it, then maybe, he could too.

All of the traits he abhorred in himself—his ambition, his intellectual interests, even his idealism—all served in her life as occasions *per accidens* of great spiritual good. Her "little way" of doing small things with great love served as a stark contrast to his own desire for grandiose moral and religious accomplishments. He described reading her autobiography as "one of the biggest and most salutary humiliations of his life"[21] for it forced him to face the reverse snobbery operating in his own exalted religious aspirations.

In November Merton returned to New York City, to work in Harlem. But he was less sure now that this was his true calling. He met with Mark Van Doren to discuss his plans and his future. Van Doren suggested that if he so willingly accepted the Franciscans' decision that he had no vocation for the priesthood, then perhaps he really didn't have one. The remark stung Merton deeply. He had been content, he tells us, to tell everybody that he had no vocation because "the drama of the rejection fueled his sense of uniqueness." It was, he said, his "way of being martyred without being martyred at all." Now Van Doren was telling him to be careful. If he kept on claiming for himself a humility even more humble than the priesthood itself, he might very well lose his vocation.[22]

Van Doren and St. Therese of Lisieux helped Merton to see that he should not give up on the priesthood. His relatively sordid past and middle-class background were not impossible barriers to living a life of religious devotion. The only thing actually holding him back was an odd attachment to his own sense of himself as somehow unworthy of his dream.

Merton spoke with a friar in New York who reassured him that his past would not prevent him from entering orders, and with renewed confidence he wrote to Gethsemani asking to make another retreat. In the letter he indicated that he would like to become a postulant. He then wrote in his journal: "Going to live in Harlem does not seem to me to be anything special. It is a good and reasonable way to follow Christ. But going to the Trappists is exciting, it fills me with awe and desire. I return to the idea again and again: 'Give up *everything, give up everything!*'"[23]

"Everything," to Merton, now meant every worldly ambition. In December he received a letter from Gethsemani accepting him and another from his draft board informing him that he had been reclassified 1-A. He got an extension on his deferment, and on December 9, 1941, he boarded the train for Trappist, Kentucky, to become a monk, less than two days after the Japanese attack on Pearl Harbor.

Chapter Three

The Monastic Turn

M erton's decision to enter the monastery was without a doubt the major turning point of his life. It sealed his shift in allegiance from the modern secular *literati* with their vague metaphysical protests—"their 'no' to everything that served as their pitiful 'yes' to themselves"—to a religious community of cloistered monks where time and transcendence merged in the holy present, and grace fell as "gratuitous as rain." Merton never thought of his decision to take Holy Orders as a retreat from the world, rather he saw it an active alternative to common conformity—a Pascalian wager of an ordinary brave man who chose internal exile rather than participate in lies or support false actions.

In later years, he questioned this rigid separation of the holy and secular realms, but at this time in his life, absolute distinctions seemed prerequisite to total commitment. And there is no doubt that his bold decision to live in total contradiction to the spirit of his times unleashed in Merton such joy and energy that from that day forward, in spite of all the difficulties, he lived a creative, joyous, spiritual life until the day he died. Just as Huck Finn had announced his willingness to go to hell if that was the price to be paid for helping a runaway slave, Merton announced, with similar conviction and foreboding, his own decision to become a monk: "You shall taste the true solitude of my anguish and my poverty and I shall lead you into the high places of my joy and you shall die in Me and find all things in My mercy which has created you for this end and brought you from Prades to Bermuda to St. Antion to Oakham to London to Cambridge to Rome to New York to Columbia to St. Bonaventure to the Cistercian Abbey of the poor men who labor in Gethsemani: 'That you may become the brother of God and learn to know the Christ of the burnt men.'"[1]

By joining the monastery Merton was setting out for new territory. But he wasn't leaving his past or the Widow Douglas behind: rather he was reconnoitering the exact location of his own denigrated religious longings by following the trail back down from the modern religious dissenters, Aldous Huxley and Jacques Maritain, through the American Transcendentalists, to their Puritan predecessors John Winthrop and William Bradford, back down to the mystics and contemplatives of the middle ages, all the way to the desert fathers— who, in their protests against the Roman Empire and the Church of Constantine had set the standard for a life lived in accord with conscience.

In monasticism, Merton believed he had found the essential tradition of the interior life—its basis and its standard. And Gethsemani seemed to him to be one of the last spots on earth where this tradition had not yet collapsed into the service of economic or political spheres or warped by the propaganda needs of nation states struggling for dominance and survival. At Gethsemani, Being had not yet been swallowed up into becoming, essence had not yet been dissolved entirely into existence, and "Newspeak" had not yet fully arrived.

Donning the monk's frock a few days after the bombing of Pearl Harbor was a lot like donning Hester Pryne's scarlet letter. It signaled both liberation and banishment, uniting Merton politically with the new Catholic immigrants who had not yet fully adapted to the American way of life and with literary eccentrics like Henry Adams and T. S. Eliot who had turned to the architecture of the medieval mind as an alternative to the materialism of their age.

But whereas Adams and Eliot had turned to the Medieval sensibility as a way of grounding their own rather sophisticated cultural analyses in historical precedents, Merton had turned to it for more personal, indeed existential reasons: to find an alternative way of life. Adams and Eliot were the aristocratic forerunners to what Norman Podhoretz would later call "the adversary culture"—a highly stylized, abstract critique of progress and modernity.[2] Merton's embrace of Cistercian spirituality was much less theoretical. His reasoning was simple: if bourgeois culture was intolerable, then leave it. If America was blind to her true spiritual heritage, then find it. And if powerlessness and poverty were the price one had to pay to fulfill one's longing for life lived in accordance with conscience, then wholeheartedly embrace them and don't look back.

If such a strategy delayed Merton's sophistication as a social critic, it nevertheless sped his development as a human being. His embrace of suffering and struggle was no mere rhetorical stance. The Trappists were a penitential order, which meant that hard physical labor was a part of the daily schedule and silence was the norm. There was no meat, fish, or eggs, and Merton would fast during Lent and Advent.[3] Every day he would rise at 2:00 A.M., go to choir, and recite Matins in honor of the Blessed Virgin Mary. Then he would spend half an hour in private meditation—kneeling or standing.

Night Office followed at 3:00 A.M. which consisted of one hour of chanting, Gospel reading, and blessing—all in Latin. Mass was said at 4:00 A.M. Afterwards there was half an hour for reading or individual prayer. Merton often used this time to write. Chapter—a kind of business meeting for the monks during which the Abbot often offered a commentary on the Rule of St. Benedict—was held at 6:00 A.M. followed by breakfast, which usually consisted of some coffee and two pieces of dry bread followed by a half hour of reading and/or study.

High Mass (Terce) came at 7:45 A.M. followed by a two-hour work period. Merton was often assigned to write Trappist tracts, hagiographies, and histories during these hours. At 11:00 A.M. there was more chanting, then dinner, usually vegetables and soup. After dinner, there was time for private prayer, reading, and study—followed by another two-hour work period.

Reading or private prayer followed until the most important prayer of the day—Vespers—was chanted at 4:30 P.M.
This was followed by a period of meditation, then light re-
freshment, followed by a half hour of private prayer, then
Compline—an antiphon chanted to the Virgin Mary an hour
before bed. The monks ended their day with an examination
of conscience, then retired at 7:00 P.M. Only to rise again at
2:00 A.M. to repeat the process.[4]

Merton's bed was a wooden bench with a straw-filled pallet
and bolster, separated from the other monks by a thin wall.
Needless to say, it was a noisy place to sleep.[5] He wore the
same robes around the clock and slept in the day's sweat.
Underclothing was changed once a week in summer, once
every two weeks in winter; showers and baths were virtually
unknown.[6]

Half the monks would be shaved on Wednesdays, the rest
on Saturdays. These were the only two days when hot water
was available. Haircuts were given once a month by two monk
barbers appointed at random. Merton could send mail only
four times a year, and two of those letters had to be sent to
family members. All mail—both incoming and outgoing—was
read by the prior.[7] There were no mirrors, no "particular
friendships." Each monk was given twenty minutes each week
to select a book from the library, which had to be approved by
the novice master.[8]

Some mitigations to these rules were beginning to come in
when Merton entered the order. He was given an extra shirt
for work, and then a work smock. Before that, while working,
the monks just fastened up the hems of their long robes with
strings. And, of course, the famous Trappist Rule of Silence
was lightened somewhat by the tradition of Trappist Sign
Language which Merton quickly mastered. "Sound" words
could only be used in an emergency.

After several months of this life, the Father Master asked
Merton if he had any thoughts about leaving the Trappists.
Merton admitted that he sometimes thought of joining the
Carthusians. The Carthusians lived in individual hermitages,
not in large dormitories, and pursued lives of greater solitude.
Without a hint of irony, Father Abbot Dom Frederic reassured

him, "Of course, you wouldn't get the penance that we have here."[9]

And yet as crazy as all this may seem to an outsider, Merton described these disciplines as effecting "a radical liberation from the delusions and obsessions of modern man and his society that preserved him from surrender of his integrity to the seductions of the totalitarian lie."[10] By "totalitarian lie" he was not just speaking of fascist or communist ideology, but of the modern psychological penchant to idolize progress and comfort over personal mastery. The totalitarian lie was the idea that the impersonal forces of history were something to be served rather than something to be resisted.

Modern civilization—and the war had exacerbated this effect—tended to value means over ends, efficiency over profundity, and quantity over quality. Progress was defined as an increase in material production, not in an increase in happiness or charity. Merton's monastic, peasant world—as he recorded it in his religious poems, hagiographies, and essays—lived by a very different set of values. It was all *end*. It was, in fact, achieving its *end* even as he groped and stumbled toward the elusive goal of total surrender to the unfathomable will of God. Daily life was a ritual of hours, and prayer a constant occupation.

Living this alternative life, keyed to the quiddities of things, was Merton's way of saying "NO to all the concentration camps, the aerial bombardments, the staged political trials, the judicial murders, the racial injustices, the economic tyrannies, and the whole socioeconomic apparatus which seems geared for nothing but global destruction in spite of all its fair words in favor of peace."[11]

And yet it is one thing to say no to aerial bombardments and another to effectively resist them. Merton may have taken the less traveled path, but he had by no means found a way to undo the worldliness of the world. That spring his brother John Paul became a sergeant in the Royal Canadian Air Force and left for England and, as it would turn out, died shortly thereafter.

For the rest of the war and for four years after the armistice, Merton did not leave the monastery except to work on the grounds.[12] Each day he followed the same strict schedule of prayer, pious reading, contemplation, manual labor, and devotion. His attention focused exclusively on attaining purity of heart.

This singularity of purpose shielded him from the temptations of a bohemian lifestyle, the narrow concerns of conventional bourgeois existence, and the disillusionments so many of his peers experienced as a result of being prematurely thrust into positions of leadership in a time of world crisis. In other words, the monastic life shielded him from cynicism and kept alive in him the humanist's hope of someday acquiring a universal perspective on existence.

During those years, Merton found that the interval after the night office, in the great silence, between four and five thirty on the mornings of feast days, was a perfect time to write verse. "After two or three hours of prayer," he notes, "your mind is saturated in peace and the richness of the liturgy. The dawn is breaking outside the cold windows. If it is warm, the birds are already beginning to sing. Whole blocks of imagery seem to crystallize out as it were naturally in the silence and the peace, and the lines almost write themselves."[13]

He struggled for a while with the notion that writing and contemplation were mutually exclusive endeavors. The writer must, for the sake of coherence, maintain his voice, and yet in contemplation, one must overcome any separation between one's self and one's experience. No matter how close the poet or writer gets to the Absolute, the mere fact that he is compelled to describe what he experiences forces him to choose independence over union. Even in profoundly spiritual writers such as Rilke and Yeats, there is this implicit alienation. Always, in the end, the poet opts for intelligibility over personal transformation; otherwise, there would be no poem. This bothered Merton, for he believed that writing mattered primarily as a means for growing a personality that in the end enabled one to transcend art.

He was finally able to reconcile these two vocations by coming to see his writing as the endless human task of correcting the misnaming of experience. Writers, like monks, helped to close the gap between knowing and being by transforming individual happenings into occasions for contemplation. Both unite the soul to its circumstances by approaching experience from a noninstrumental point of view. Poetry, like prayer, tempers self-centeredness and reorients perception by decentering the ego and revealing the value of things as ends in themselves. Like scripture, it educates the imagination by synthesizing the concrete with the abstract into a new category of knowing: the symbolic.

In the symbolic realm our radically contingent lives become part of larger, universal patterns, and our subjective experiences find their context in a time outside of time. History may be written by the victors, but poetry is written by displaced persons: survivors, nonconformists, and guilty bystanders—those beaten but not yet bowed individuals isolated or exiled from the common commerce, politics, and fashions of their day. Another way of saying this is that poetry does not provide an interpretation of history; it is an attempt to overcome it. Poetry shows us how human subjectivity can resist time, frame its own context, and trope the tropes attempting to define it from without. It does not teach us the meaning of the past but rather its value as seen in the light of an autonomous presence always already transcendent to it. Poetry is, in a nutshell, the living expression of an eschatological counterculture.

In 1942 Merton published a poem in *Poetry* magazine and the next year another poem in the *New Yorker*. Mark Van Doren sent them to James Laughlin at New Directions, and so thanks to Van Doren, Merton's first book *Thirty Poems* was published in 1944. The best poem in this collection was "For My Brother: Reported Missing in Action, 1943."

Just before his brother was killed, Merton had been reading his letters from the front and noticed a sudden inability to talk about what he was seeing. Merton interpreted this to mean that "John Paul had at last come face to face with the world that he and I had helped to make!"[14] The poem expresses this sense of shared helplessness and culpability.

Sweet Brother, if I do not sleep
My eyes are flowers for your tomb;
And if I cannot eat my bread,
My fasts shall live like willows where you died.

What is remarkable here is Merton's assumption that his path and his brother's had not diverged at all. Both of them—the soldier and the monk—were living lives of Christian sacrifice that required privations, self-abnegations, even the acceptance of death. Both had crosses to bear and obligations to meet.

When all the men of war are shot
And flags have fallen into dust,
Your cross and mine shall tell men still
Christ died on each, for both of us.

For in the wreckage of your April Christ lies/slain,
And Christ weeps in the ruins of my spring.[15]

This first volume of poetry contained a few other war-inspired poems, as well as autobiographical and religious meditations on such topics as "The Evening of the Visitation," "The Blessed Virgin Mary Compared to a Window," and "The Sponge Full of Vinegar." These poems explored Christian themes using surrealist language. They yoked orthodoxy to modernity at the level of psychological revelation. But except for the one poem about his brother, the brutality of the war, its grandeur, and the desperation of Merton's own spiritual life, got buried beneath all the culture and history he was carrying.

Merton's second volume of poetry *Man in a Divided Sea* (1946) continued in the same vein with poems about "Ash Wednesday," "Trappists Working," and "The Blessed Sacrament," as well as a few on classical themes such as "The Oracle," "Calypso's Island," and "The Pride of the Dead." Catholic iconography still dominated his imagination, serving as an aid to reflection but also limiting the range of his line.

Consider for example this section from his poem "The House of Caiphas."

> Somewhere, inside the wintry colonnade,
> Stands, like a churchdoor statue, God's Apostle,
> Good St. Peter, by the brazier,
> With his back turned to the trail.
>
> As scared and violent as flocks of birds of prey,
> The testimonies of the holy beggars
> Fly from the stones, and scatter in the windy shadows.[16]

The imagery here is compelling, especially the "testimony of the beggars" flying from the stones to scatter in the wind. In that line the joy Merton found in his holy vow of poverty leaps from the page, and we begin to experience what he has accomplished as a cloistered monk.

But that's part of the problem. What leaps from the page is his experience of orthodoxy. The poems surprise us with unexpected applications of traditional church doctrines. But once we know the game, their ingenious connections no longer strike us as original discoveries but as illustrations of acquired principles.

At Columbia, Mark Van Doren had saved Merton from the snobbery of the French lycee and the priggishness of Cambridge, opening him up to a living literary tradition. Merton was writing Emersonian poems on monasticism. But given the pervasive influence of T. S. Eliot and Allan Tate on his generation of poets, he tended to overload them with religious allusions and classical learning. If there were flashes of brilliance, these flashes were dulled by the machinery of doctrine. And so in the end, most of these early poems, like so many other "religious verses," fail. There is simply too much incense in the air.

But *Figures for an Apocalypse*, published in 1947 overcame many of these problems and signaled a shift in both Merton's style and sensibility. The themes are familiar but the tone is less pious, and the language more vital. The content also anticipates Merton's later move into explicit social criticism.

These poems were not written by a coy monk who had found God by leaving the world, but rather by a suffering servant who found himself in as much spiritual peril as the rest of us. Notice the independence in these lines:

> How can we make our way to where you are
> Facing all day the innocent terror
> That shadows us behind this cliff?
> What eyes we seem to feel
> Reaching toward our backs as frail as tentacles:
> Eyes that we turn to face, and never see![17]

In these new poems Merton also expressed outrage at what was happening in the world. "The bureaucrats, wiping the blood off their fingers / In the gates of the Temple of Reason / Have voted to poison the enemy's well."[18]

From time to time he even lapsed into harangues against millionaires, limousines, and mass culture with all the invective of a Gregory Corso or Allen Ginsberg. "Do your forgotten movies still distill those tears of ice? / Fasten no more these pilgrims to your clock-work heart / Nor press them to the beats that tick behind your scribbled walls / Where all your somber ways are a dead end!" (Poems 189).

Figures for an Apocalypse demonstrated that Merton was moving toward a more unfettered dialogue with the world and that he was bringing his Catholicism with him—not as historical and cultural baggage, but as part of a unique and evolving countercultural point of view.

T. S. Eliot read this collection and found it hit or miss. "Too much writing and too little revision," he quipped.[19] But Merton felt he had turned a corner. He no longer saw any conflict between being a writer and being a monk; in fact the two complemented one another. "If in the past I have desired to stop writing," he observed, "I can see now that it is much better for me to go on trying to learn to write under the strange conditions imposed by Cistercian life. I can become a saint by writing well for the glory of God."[20]

It was at this time that Merton began to correspond directly with James Laughlin at New Directions over the possibility of writing something "like a cross between Dante's Purgatory, and Kafka, and a medieval miracle play, called *The Seven Storey Mountain.*"[21]

The book quickly became straight autobiography "with a lot of comment and reflection."[22] Merton was excited by the fact that the book seemed to be taking off in his hands, unlike his novels. And although his poetry often seemed to write itself, when it did, he admitted, it came from a source other than creative inspiration, something more akin to autohypnosis.

The Seven Storey Mountain, on the other hand, emerged from some deeper and more universal source right from the start. Merton ended up publishing it with Harcourt Brace rather than New Directions and took out several key sections relating to his experiences at Cambridge, which are now lost. But when it was finally published in 1948, Merton's newfound voice—half modern/half cloistered—sparkled on every page. The book immediately became an international best seller.

Its critical reception, although respectful, was less enthusiastic. Reviewers always have difficulty with religious books. Many are simply offended by such outright declarations of faith, while others are secretly thrilled. But most simply refuse to be impressed one way or another. This is why religious books tend to get less critical attention than they usually deserve. *The Seven Storey Mountain* was no exception. Its style was praised but its content largely ignored, and its vast popularity was regarded as a bit of a scandal.

Still it was one of those books written in poverty and obscurity by a man who knew who he was, and, therefore, could afford to wait. Its philosophical importance emerged only over time. In fact, I believe its true intellectual significance has yet to be fully understood.

Chapter Four

The Seven Storey Mountain

O ne way to read *The Seven Storey Mountain* is as a vast moral reclamation project in which Merton defends the Christian verities against the fashionable naturalism and positivist pieties of his day and in the process forges for himself an ethic to live by. Monasticism provided him with a vantage point from which to see through the Kitsch, Camp, terror, and sentimentality of his times. But it also revealed to him new responsibilities as a watchman and a critic. The deeper he moved into his faith, the deeper he moved into a recognition of hitherto unimagined social and spiritual obligations.

Of course, other postwar writers had similar stories to tell. James Baldwin, J. D. Salinger, Philp Roth, and Ralph Ellison all plumbed the depths of their own personal religious histories for clues as to how to survive in an increasingly impersonal world teeming with antagonisms toward traditional plebeian values. Unlike Merton, however, these writers moved more fully into secular existence, abandoning traditional religious ideas as ill adapted to the realities of the age.

Merton, by contrast, embraced religious faith and identified with the critiques of postindustrial society offered by various displaced refugee intellectuals such as Paul Tillich, Erich Fromm, and Hannah Arendt. He shared their sense of historical discontinuity, their sense of living in a cultural Diaspora. But he did not share their religious skepticism. The confident tone of his autobiography signaled an end to his sense of spiritual isolation. He was a *finder* now—not a *seeker*—living outside of time in the country of the "burnt men" and the crucified Christ. He had stopped worrying about how to live and had begun living on grace—luxuriating in his alienation as only a Trappist Monk or a demigod might.

Part of the book's appeal for non-Catholics came from the fact that Merton presented essentialist church doctrines in less ethnocentric, more existential terms. The autobiographical genre helped here, for in the context of the story of Merton's own evolving character, terms like *sacrament*, *divinity*, even *contemplation* became poetic images for personal psychological states. This opened Catholic theology to the culture at large—not by watering down its doctrines or emphasizing its continuities with mainstream Protestantism (as Fulton Sheen did in his best-seller *Peace of Soul*, published just one year later) but by translating its rigorous ascetic traditions into the language of contemporary experience.

The book is divided into three parts. Part 1 explores the insufficiencies of human aspirations. It is a lyric confession of loneliness and inner grief that culminates with the death of Merton's grandfather in 1936, followed by Merton's youthful recognition of the futility of a life of self-seeking.

Part 2 explores the revelations that emerge once Merton accepts the fact that human nature, by itself, can do little to settle life's most important problems. "If we follow nothing but our natures, our own philosophies, our own level of ethics," he tells us, "we will end up in hell. This would be a depressing thought if it were not purely abstract. Because in the concrete order of things God gave man a nature that was ordered to a supernatural life."[1] This section ends with Merton's decision to become a priest.

Part 3 narrates the unfolding of several specific spiritual discoveries as Merton follows the pull of "Magnetic North" toward the supernatural life. This section ends with his brother's death in 1943 and with Merton accepting despair, ingesting his grief, and acknowledging his own part in the world's sorrows. Like Alyosha in the *Brothers Karamazov*, he decides to live like a monk in the world; only for Merton this means that he must *really be a monk* and confront the world with the radical alternative of his own complete and total religious dissent.

The book concludes with an Epilogue "Meditatio Pauperis in Solitudine." This section describes what life is like lived on the far side of worldly ambition. Here "Christ pours down the Holy Ghost upon you from heaven in the fire of June, and then you look about you and realize that you are standing in the barnyard husking corn, and the cold wind of the last days of October is sweeping across the thin woods and biting you to the bone. And then, in a minute or so, it is Christmas, and Christ is born."[2] Here the circle is completed, Merton's ego dissolves into his higher Self, which in turn dissolves into a love for the world.

The Seven Storey Mountain is, in essence, an orthodox counterpoint to James Joyce's *Portrait of the Artist as a Young Man* and to all the other twentieth-century *bildungsromans* that celebrate emancipation from tradition, family, state, and religion. Unlike those tales of self-discovery through exile and rebellion, Merton describes his own liberation as a discovery of a deep continuity with the spiritual traditions of the past. He does not seek this out for the sake of mere solace or reactionary energy, but as a stay against the disorienting and fragmenting forces of contemporary existence. Monasticism is a kind of instinctual flinch at the culture of modernity, a life-preserving, involuntary recoil from civilization as we know it.

The book's stylistic strength comes from the equanimity and candor of Merton's voice: a voice poised in the world but not of it. He describes with precision his own fallen existence from the detached perspective of someone who has died to the values of this world. Although his story has a classic dramatic arc—little boy lost becomes little boy found—its shifting focus from fallen consciousness to redeemed perception takes place primarily at the paragraph level. This may account for the book's rare combination of lyric intensity and intellectual power. For if lyricism is primarily a quality of the sentence, at the paragraph level different ideas enter into conversation with one another until one clearly amended, properly qualified claim emerges. The momentum from paragraph to paragraph—like that experienced in contemplation—is toward ever greater accuracy and specificity. Ideas are not synthesized or overcome in any Hegelian "sublation," but rather brought down to cases and painstakingly particularized until the reader is taken up into the ongoing conversation between Merton's self and Merton's soul.

The Seven Storey Mountain resonated powerfully with those looking for a nonmaterialistic, nonscientific alternative to the ideologies of the new super states. To meet the dangerous new power alignments of the postwar world, a new America had emerged—corporate, consolidated, internationally connected, and militarily ready, run by professional managers, social scientists, and experts. The most pressing question of the era was not how the country's unique democratic character was going to be preserved, but rather whose interests this new class of technocrats were going to serve.

Merton offered a refreshingly frank answer to this question. The new class would serve exactly the same worldly values as the old ones: progress, money, power, and development. The allies' victory saved the world from entering a new dark age, but if we failed to recognize the empty cultural forms that had preceded the war and that threatened again to follow in its wake, then there was a very real danger that victory could become hollow.

The Seven Storey Mountain, by examining the place of mysticism in history, or rather by examining its "absence," raised the questions of the role of individual conscience in the new technological society. Merton, more or less, agreed with Mahatma Gandhi, that history was "the record of every interruption of the even working of the force of love."[3] It represented everything that was not essential, everything that stood between the individual and God. It was an account— and this was confirmed by the experiences of the G.I.s now returning home—of the accumulated sins of the fathers visited upon the sons, shadows playing upon the inside of a cave; a nightmare from which we were continually trying to awake.

And yet, for Merton and Gandhi, human experience, existential reality, events were no mere fictions. If life's time-bound particulars sometimes obscured their transcendental source, and if the chronicles of human strife often hid the mystery of existence behind a veil of self-justifications, that did not mean that Reality itself could not be known. Only that it was usually misnamed. And it was in this process of misnaming that the significance of experience itself got fatally distorted, causing individuals to oscillate between personal preoccupation with their own subjective experiences and a pseudoscientific materialism posited as a presupposition for conventional sanity.

As the allusion to Dante in the title implies, *The Seven Storey Mountain* represented the modern world as a purgatory—a spiritual Diaspora where the most profound human values and experiences were rapidly being exiled, left for dead, or buried at sea. Western civilization, in an instinctual rejoinder to the militarism of the emerging totalitarian states, had itself embraced the values of production, consumption, and military might. In the process it had lost track of its single greatest strength: the ascetic ideal.

If Western civilization was going to survive, Merton's book suggested, it would have to go inward, monastic, and get back in touch with the spirit of self-renunciation. Protestant America in its conversation with Enlightenment skepticism had accepted the epistemological preoccupations of the new sciences as central—concerning itself with evidences and theological proofs, but never fully coming to grips with the wisdom tradition still lurking within the Medieval imagination. This rootless, invented, Protestant American self longed for a spiritual home, but given its preoccupation with Cartesian certainties had no means for arriving there.

The contemplative tradition—updated by a healthy dose of existentialism—could bring the Western religious imagination back in touch with its deeper self and go beyond William James's focus on the philosophical reasonableness and moral helpfulness of faith, to the "absolutely, paradoxically, teleologically placed" ecstasy of the apostle. American believers, Merton insisted, had to look to Emerson, Dickinson, Whitman, and Thoreau for models of prophetic faith. And then they had to act on their discoveries *by living alternative lives*.

Asceticism, as Merton understood it, was not a denial of the body but its fulfillment in active virtue. It was heroism experienced from the inside out, self-sacrifice internalized and thereby overcome, the ego ideal reconciled with both the superego and the id. Norman O. Brown later argued that the entire sweep of Western religious orthodoxy was based upon a neurotic denial of the pleasures of the body. For him, the psychoanalytic meaning of history was found in the struggle of the socially constructed self against Holy Polymorphus Perversity, the true source of oceanic oneness and selfless love. But Merton, although he would have agreed that the real history of mankind was hidden in the internal struggle of the psyche against itself, would never have characterized that struggle as a fight between the spirit and the body. This was simply a common misconception. Asceticism, as William Blake had taught him, was a liberation of the body not only from the false commands of the ego and superego, but also from the equally dictatorial demands of the id. The goal of the interior life was not a return to or an abandonment of the physical joys of existence, but rather freedom from any prior claims on the spirit and the soul.

Surprisingly the sharpest criticism of Merton's views came from a fellow Benedictine monk, Dom Aelred Graham, who would later become a close friend of Merton's and author of the influential book *Zen Catholicism* (1963). Graham's biting critique of *The Seven Storey Mountain* published in *Atlantic Monthly* in 1953 was titled "A Modern Man in Reverse." In that piece, he argued that Merton's "mysticism for the masses" constituted a retreat from the world at the very moment when what the world really needed was Christian action. Graham remarked: "One element of popular success in Merton's writing may be its power to bring vicarious satisfaction to those who remain in normal society yet share his indignation at its evils, a pleasing sense of being on the side of the angels. Denunciation of the unregenerate 'they' is only one step removed from 'I am holier than thou.'"[4]

But Merton did not see himself as advocating quietism or world renunciation. He saw the monastic life as serving an important public function: it provided an alternative reading of contemporary events from the far side of history. In fact, in 1954—a year after Graham's review was published—Merton wrote a letter to Erich Fromm noting the similarities between psychoanalysis and spiritual direction as suprahistorical disciplines and asked Fromm if he would like to begin a dialogue over the direction modern civilization seemed to be taking. "At a time like the present," Merton wrote, "when over vast areas of the earth systems of thought and government are tending to the complete debasement of man's fundamental dignity as the image of God, it seems to me important that all who take to heart the value and the nobility of the human spirit should realize their solidarity with one another, and should be able to communicate with one another in every way, in spite of perhaps grave doctrinal divergences."[5]

What Merton was getting at here was that the image of man in *The Seven Storey Mountain* as a creature made in God's image, given free will and capable of the experience of divine grace, had been replaced by an image of man as an ensemble of social relations. In the end this operational definition would undermine Western civilization's capacity to assert any universality for its moral aims. The danger wasn't that Americans would turn *en masse* to contemplative living— as Graham had argued—abandoning their world historical role as defenders of human rights and individual autonomy. The danger was that they might worship the false god of prosperity and thereby abandon the aspiration to forge a life lived in accord with conscience. Postwar America, in other words, might fall to the apostasy of materialism and idolize its technicians and experts as a prophetic minority destined to redeem the world.

Merton did not believe that this was leading to a clash between myths—materialism verses monasticism—but to something far more subtle and divisive: a clash between versions of the same myth—a veritable metaphysical civil war with both sides considering themselves the true heirs of the America Dream. One side seeking self-realization, the other self-transcendence; one side desiring to wield power, the other to radiate it. In the coming decades this conflict would play itself out in the cultural civil war of the 1960s as Merton applied his personalistic, spiritual world view to questions of American public policy. But at the time *The Seven Storey Mountain* was published, he was seen merely as a sweet monk understandably out of touch with the demands of realpolitik—tolerated, as most mystics are tolerated, as a kind of forgivable extremist. And yet for those with religious longing, *The Seven Storey Mountain* offered an exciting new possibility: inspired, fervent *nonconformity*.

CHAPTER FIVE

NEW SEEDS OF CONTEMPLATION

I n the years directly after the publication of *The Seven Storey Mountain*, Merton published a series of Trappist tracts: *Exile Ends in Glory, Seeds of Contemplation, The Waters of Siloe, What Are These Wounds?* and *The Ascent to Truth*. Most of these books had been written over the last ten years by order of the Abbot. Needless to say, their publication in no way broadened Merton's popular appeal.

It may sound odd to say it, but *The Seven Storey Mountain* was a kind of public philosopher's swan song. Its message: Real life is elsewhere, in silence and in solitude. Every book Merton published after it was essentially a gloss on this theme: a qualification, an extension, a rejoinder, or a rearticulation. Merton seemed content in his role as outsider and "marginal man." And yet events were conspiring to extend his public influence. The Abbey at Gethsemani began to modernize its production facility becoming more of a working farm. The number of novices grew along with Merton's fame, and as the place got busier, Merton did too. He began to crave more solitude. In fact, he even looked into transferring to the Carthusians again.

The Abbot, recognizing Merton's need for more privacy, gave him a small shed to serve as a hermitage, and Merton christened it St. Anne's. It was there that Merton began to write a series of books on the nature of solitude that would transform the world's understanding of the nature and meaning of monasticism.

In 1948, he published *Seeds of Contemplation* with New Directions. It was a series of notes "like Pascal's Pensees" designed to serve as an aid to spiritual reflection. Merton claimed no originality for the book, insisting that it was simply a transcription of what many other cloistered monks lived and already knew. But the experimental format and the psychological probity of his remarks led a few Cistercians to disavow its orthodoxy. Apparently, Merton's views were less mainstream than he thought.

The very next year he began to work on a book of formal theology, eventually published as *The Ascent to Truth* in 1951. In this book Merton tried to synthesize the experiential spirituality of the mystics with the formal intellectual structures of Saint Thomas Aquinas. It was the closest he ever came to articulating a theological system. And although it impressed other religious thinkers—especially those Buddhist monks who were looking for links with Western religions—unlike *The Seven Storey Mountain*, it was an insider's text, a mystic's treatise, an intellectual exercise in scholastic clarification. And the times seemed to be calling for something else, something different.

Merton took a second look at *Seeds of Contemplation* and found that its focus upon prayer and the contemplative life offered a more thoroughgoing spiritual interpretation of the world than straight theology. So he revised *Seeds*, and in the process created a bold new genre that was part reflection, part exhortation, and part social critique.

The revised version of *Seeds of Contemplation* was, in other words, a literary breakthrough. Merton's Desert Spirituality had found its psychological idiom. He now wrote "about spiritual things from the point of view of experience rather than in the concise terms of dogmatic theology or metaphysics."[1] This explicit focus upon the concrete, the contingent, and the actual—already implicit in his autobiography—allowed Merton to sidestep the theologians' need for a system, and by so doing overcome the paralysis inherent in the prevailing religious debates over first premises.

By beginning at the level of experience rather than doctrine, Merton was able, like William James, to redefine religious ideas in light of their *use*. This made it possible for him to bring Catholic theology into dialogue with other religions and secular thought without getting hung up on semantic distinctions. Unlike William James, however, he made no case for the reasonableness of faith; rather his focus was upon its prophetic capacity to deepen and extend the meaning of everyday experience. Monasticism, in other words, offered its practitioners more than just perceptual reorientation; it constituted a kind of psychological Copernican revolution.

With this turn, Merton began to exploit more fully the strength he had always possessed as a writer but had hitherto only sporadically employed: his capacity to render refined religious concepts in the language of everyday experience. But even more than that, he had a original interpretation of contemporary alienation. The spiritual isolation we all experience as moderns, he argued, came from a renunciation of solitude.

The popularizers of positive thinking—by counseling a retreat from existential anxiety into autohypnosis—were only making matters worse. "Place no hope in the inspirational preachers of Christian sunshine," Merton warned, "who are able to pick you up and set you back on your feet and make you feel good for three or four days—until you fold up and collapse into despair."

"Self-confidence," he explained, "is a precious natural gift, a sign of health. But it is not the same thing as faith. Faith is much deeper, and it must be deep enough to subsist when we are weak, when we are sick, when our self-confidence is gone, when our self-respect is gone. I do not mean that faith only functions when we are otherwise in a state of collapse. But true faith must be able to go on even when everything else is taken away from us. Only a humble man is able to accept faith on these terms, so completely without reservation that he is glad of it in its pure state, and welcomes it happily even when nothing else comes with it, and when everything else is taken away."[2]

Only the more rigorous forms of spiritual religion offered hope for keeping faith alive amid all the substitute gratifications of the consumer society.[3] Asceticism, the soul of monasticism, functioned as a form of ethical rehabilitation. It was, Merton explained, a strategy for undercutting the ubiquitous influence of the market, the media, and the masses. By returning to the teachings of the Desert Fathers, we could return to the wellsprings of Christian cultural resistance.

In the spring of 1950, *Partisan Review* held a symposium on "Religion and the Intellectuals" in which John Dewey characterized the postwar religious turn in America as symptomatic of a "loss of intellectual nerve." It grew, he argued, out of despair over our inability to reform the world, and it was evidence of national immaturity. Instead of a return to religion, he argued, what was really needed was a spirited debate over public policy and a rebirth of the pragmatic liberalism of FDR's New Deal.

But, for Merton, such criticism—given the events of the last ten years—was itself symptomatic of another kind of loss of nerve: a refusal to face up to the lessons of the Holocaust, Hiroshima, and the two world wars, to own up to the radical truth that we have become moral and intellectual dwarfs overwhelmed by the power of our machines, active participants in the worldwide triumph of a technologically enhanced militarism. To embrace new methods, arrangements, or political strategies as *the solution* to this startling new state of affairs was itself a retreat into technique and method and away from responsibility.

The prevailing hubris was that science precluded hubris. The new technocrats had become blind to their illusions because they believed they had seen through the illusions of other men and, because they did not worship other men's idols, they believed they had none of their own. This kind of intellectual complacency and moral blindness, hidden as it was beneath a flurry of activism, was not easy to expose because it did not see itself as complacent, but radically self-critical. True, at the level of process and method, the new pragmatists appeared profoundly, theoretically self-conscious; but they lacked a full critique of their ultimate ends and governing *telos*.

For Thomas Merton World War II had been a massive, global affliction so virulent that the Western Allies began to manifest some of the same traits as their enemies: most notably a need for control and a focus upon strategic interests over principles. If the country was ever to going to meet the challenge posed by totalitarian states without itself becoming totalitarian, it would need a moral perspective less shrill than the apocalyptic vision of the Cold Warriors, but less "cool" than the new managerial middle class.

Into this breach leapt a new breed of public intellectuals—Reinhold Niebuhr, Lewis Mumford, Edmund Wilson, Dwight Macdonald, and, most notably, Lionel Trilling—who took it upon themselves to articulate a middle ground. Professor Trilling was particularly representative of this effort in that he explicitly tried to thaw the middle-brow mentality of the managerial classes though a renewal of liberal education. Matthew Arnold had shown him the way. If the culture of expertise lacked soul, one could initiate the experts into a tragic sense of life!

Reinhold Niebuhr admired Trilling's efforts to reform higher education, but he went one step further. Niebuhr was not content merely to "Hellenize the new Philistines." He wanted to bring home to them an Hebraic sense of moral obligation. Without a sense of history, the new bourgeois tech-nocrats and managers just might put the country's great wealth and power in the service of their own petty dreams for comfort and control. Niebuhr encouraged them to take upon themselves the burden of an authentic "Christian realism." That is to say, he argued that to be a moral man in an immoral world, one had to face up to the paradox, made plain by the war, that sometimes one had to do evil in order to accomplish good.

But Merton considered both of these positions as disingen-uous compromises that betrayed Gospel values. It wasn't just the management class or the ruling elites that were under-mining democratic ideals, it was the triumph of instrumental-ist thought born of materialist premises that was infecting virtually every level of society with the virus of amorality. This plague—which rapidly progressed from cynicism to nihilism—had infected the socialists as completely as it had the capitalists and had corrupted the workers as profoundly as it had the owners. Educating the public into ironies and paradoxes—as advanced by these new critics and public intellectuals—was not enough to direct a nation already disoriented by the propaganda barrage of World War II. And Niebuhr's "Christian realism" pitched to this same reeling postwar population only served to justify a tendency to shoot first and ask questions later.

The contrast between Niebuhr and Merton is particularly instructive. Niebuhr was the single most influential religious intellectual in postwar America. He embraced the paradoxes of modern Christianity as powerfully as Merton—insisting that there could be no salvation in human history and yet no grace apart from it. But ultimately the kind of activist public intellectual he became was the very antithesis of Merton's monastic "marginal man." Merton, remember, spent over a third of his day in prayer and silence, while Niebuhr attended conferences, met with public officials, published rejoinders to public policy statements, and made himself heard in the corridors of power. Niebuhr spent forty weekends a year traveling around the country giving sermons and making sure his "realist" Christian morality entered into the public debates of his day.

Merton, on the other hand, retired from the world, lived the life of a peasant, kept close to nature and solitude, and eventually even became a hermit. He played down the public acclaim, the business of an "important man," for the duties of a monk to teach, to serve, to work, to pray, and to stay close to the poor. For him, the first duty of the Christian apostle was to *practice* what he preached, not become a *spokesman* for a "Christian world view." As a result, Merton's vows of poverty, chastity, and obedience put him in a much more radical relationship to his times than Niebuhr, who may have been a more consistent social theorist but did live an alternative way of life.

And yet Merton, like Niebuhr, understood the dangers of too onesided a rejection of the world. He too advocated a tragic awareness of man's limitations. He too took the "long view." But Merton's public work was more "private," if I can put it that way. He addressed specific individuals through personal correspondence and conversation. And he wrote books for ordinary men and women seeking wholeness in a fragmented age. He did not write—as Niebuhr did—"with one eye firmly fixed on social and political forces."[4] He wrote directly to other disoriented modern souls with one ear tuned to the silence.

Another way of putting this is that while Niebuhr moved beyond tragedy to point out the "ironies" of American history, Merton threw his life into the mystic, contemplative abyss in order to reveal our hypocrisies and complicities. Merton wasn't as interested in distinguishing between the lesser of two political evils as he was in describing the impact our politicized world was having upon our ability to attain purity of heart.

CHAPTER SIX

MERTON AS EDUCATOR

In 1951 Merton was named Master of the Scholastics at Gethsemani. This made him the academic advisor and spiritual director for those preparing for ordination. He took this appointment very seriously and mentions it often in his letters. In *Sign of Jonas*, his journal from these years, he describes his new position as placing him on the threshold of a whole new existence.

"It is as if I were beginning all over again to be a Cistercian," he wrote, "but this time I am doing it without asking myself the abstract questions which are the luxury and the torment of one's monastic adolescence. For now I am a grown-up monk and have no time for anything but the essentials. The only essential is not an idea or an ideal: it is God Himself, Who cannot be found by weighing the present against the future or the past but only by sinking into the heart of the present as it is."[1]

Merton's new responsibilities forced him to reconsider his monastic vocation in terms of its social function. He began to see himself more clearly as an intellectual worker with obligations vis-à-vis the secular world. Monastic formation was a form of cultural demystification.

In *The Seven Storey Mountain* Merton had spoken ruefully of his flirtation with psychotherapy while in college. But his role as spiritual advisor to the novices forced him to take a second look at Freud, Rank, and Jung. In fact, Merton later even wrote an essay titled "Neurosis in Monastic Life," which explored the relationship between religion and the unconscious and led to his infamous encounter with the Catholic psychoanalyst Gregory Zilboorg. Zilboorg accused Merton of wanting to be a hermit just so long as his hermitage was in Time's Square with a neon sign rising above it announcing "Hermit Lives Here."

Zilboorg told Merton that his desire to write was evidence of an inability to commit himself to monasticism and charged him with personal inauthenticity. Merton was deeply insulted by these remarks, but agreed to undergo psychotherapy when he got back to Kentucky. The therapist found Merton a psychologically integrated man, not at all inauthentic, and Merton kept right on writing. Indeed he now wrote with even greater conviction.

Although he was fascinated by psychoanalysis, Merton never accepted the materialist premises or implicit naturalism of orthodox Freudianism. For him the "unconscious" remained just another introjection of the "social" self—not "primary material." Our true self—our mystic core—is supraconscious. And so although psychoanalysis has much to tell us about the many levels upon which our false selves operate, it can never tell us who we really are. As novice master, Merton's job was to nurture whatever seeds of transcendence God himself had planted in the souls of the students, not tear down their defenses in order to reconstruct their egos in line with some religious ideal.

"The worth and meaning of every ascetic practice," Merton explained, "is to be estimated in terms of quietude, lucidity of spirit, love, and purity of heart. Anything that does not lead to these is worthless, for instead of liberating us from self-preoccupation, it only reinforces our illusory and obsessive concern with our own ego and its victory over the 'not-I'. True quietude and purity of heart are impossible where this division of the 'I' (considered as right and good) and the 'not-I' (considered as threatening) governs our conduct and our decisions. . . .When one has been liberated from this obsession with self . . . one attains to integrity, to the 'conduct of the new man.' This is the 'beginning' of the true life, the life of interior or spiritual man who lives entirely as a son of God and not as a slave."[2]

Once this ascent from slave morality begins and there is a willingness on the part of the novice to face the interior void, then he begins to hear what his spiritual master has to teach him—but not before. "No one teaches contemplation," Merton points out, "except God, Who gives it. The best you can do is write something or say something that will serve as an occasion for someone else to realize what God wants of him."[3]

The primary problem for the novices, Merton believed, had chiefly to do with "thoughts"—useless interior activity and self-projections into words and ideas. By submitting to the authority of a spiritual director, the novices could protect themselves from certain common idolatries. The director reassured them that their minds—although they appeared full—were really empty, and that at the center of this nothingness was something infinitely real.

The spiritual director's job was to persuade the novice to quit trying to run his own life with the meager resources of his own mind. Only then could he take consolations from God—consolations so profound that one was usually uneasy talking about them because they often could not even be expressed. Merton cites the Desert Father's ennumeration of the stages of spiritual growth: "Renunciation of the love of money is the beginning of the conduct of the interior man. Then (renunciation) of praise. Then humility, patience, and *the vigilance of noble concerns*."[4] One doesn't acquire moral virtue by learning the various systems of moral philosophy. Spiritual direction is a tempering of the will—an initiation into the vigilance of "noble concerns."

Novices are often attracted to curious new methods and novel doctrines, Merton explains, because such innovations are outlets for self-will. But the novice master must see through these interests and continue to advocate humility and patience. Moreover, he must persist when the student's self-will transforms itself into self-justification, and then finally into the desire to please. The director does not want to place the novice under his will but to develop in him an unshakable indifference to both censure and praise.

James Finley, one of Merton's students and now a clinical psychologist, put it this way: "Merton's message is that every Christian, in his own way as willed by God, must by way of simple faith, selfless love, and humble prayer realize that the nothingness he fears is in fact the treasure he longs for."[5] He must learn to expect nothing out of anything, and everything out of nothing.

"The fruit of education," Merton wrote, "whether in the university (as for Eckhart) or in the monastery (as for Ruysbroeck) is the activation of that inmost center, that *scintilla animae*, that 'apex' or 'spark' which is a freedom beyond freedom, an identity beyond essence, a self beyond all ego, a being beyond the created realm, and a consciousness that transcends all separation. To activate this spark is not to be, like Plotinus, 'alone with the Alone,' but to recognize the Alone which is by itself in everything because there is nothing that can be with It, and nothing that can realize It. It can only realize itself.

"The 'spark', our true self, is the flash of the Absolute recognizing itself in the individual student. The purpose of all learning is to dispose the individual for this, and the purpose of various disciplines is to provide paths which lead to this ignition. The whole purpose of life is to learn how to ignite this spark without dependence on any specific external means."[6]

What is remarkable about this formulation is not its newness but its freshness. These ideas have been around for a long time, but few have been able to articulate them to a twentieth-century readership with as much power, precision, confidence, or commitment as Thomas Merton. His writings on education and spiritual direction are not works of theology proper but rather a new species of "Zen" rhetoric designed to facilitate the unlearning of false antinomies and unnecessary philosophical oppositions.

Here Merton drew on Cistercian Tradition, especially the writings of Adam of Perseigne, a twelfth-century novice master and abbot, who wrote a treatise titled "The Feast of Freedom: Monastic Formation According to Adam of Perseigne."[7] In that work Perseigne described education as a drawing out of the inner spiritual form implanted in the disciple's soul by grace. It was not a matter of imposing a rigid and artificial form from without, but of encouraging the radiation of light within the soul, until this light gained possession of the novice's whole being, informed all his actions, and bore witness to Christ living in him.

John Howard Griffin tells the story of a young Southern minister who came to Merton in the mid-sixties asking him what he should do about segregation in the churches in his area. Merton told him, "Don't do a damn thing. Take the time to become what you profess to be. Then you will know what to do."[8]

One might object that if one took that much time, no one would ever do anything since we are never fully ourselves. We can remove mask after mask, and still not arrive at an identity secure enough to justify any moral choice. Still, let's not miss Merton's point. We need not have hit the bedrock of some final identity before we act. But if we ask another what we should do, that is clearly a symptom that we cannot yet choose in good faith.

When John Paul Sartre was asked by a young man whether he should take care of his sick mother or join the resistance, his legendary reply was, "Choose! That is to say, create!" But such an answer from Merton's point of view begs the question because it doesn't recognize that authenticity resides in recognizing the inevitable falseness of *all* our subjective choices. Every choice we make is partial, a product of incapacity, for our fallen souls are in perpetual need of instruction and moral correction.

"Our false selves," Merton warns, are "the persons we want ourselves to be but who cannot exist because God does not know anything about them."[9] They are the pretender selves who exist in a world of fantasy and illusion, outside the reach of God's will and God's love—outside all of life's demands for unseen sacrifices. To let this self choose would be pure folly.

And yet, Merton tells us, "For most people in the world there is no greater subjective reality than this false self of theirs, which cannot exist. A life devoted to the cult of this shadow is what is called a life of sin."[10] The problems blocking effective social reform do not come from a lack of ideas about how things should be changed; everyone has their solutions. They derive from the fragmentation that results from a multiplicity of passionately held superficial cures. And so, before any meaningful change can occur, someone needs to articulate a deeper shared reality that is more than just a set of proffered political compromises or appeals to enlightened self-interest.

Merton's entire life was a search for that deeper reality. As a teacher and spiritual director, he was less concerned with apologetics than with purity of heart. Those who entered the monastery with a stoic contempt for worldly values had it only half right. By turning away from the materialism and cheap emotion of American cultural kitsch with heroic despair, they bravely sought God in a desert where the emotions could find nothing to sustain them. "But this too can be an error," Merton pointed out. "For if our emotions really die in the desert, our humanity dies with them. We must return from the desert like Jesus or St. John, with our capacity for feeling expanded and deepened, strengthened against the appeals of falsity, warned against temptation, great, noble and pure."[11]

This *return from the desert* was to become one of Merton's great themes as a spiritual director. One's decision to join the Trappists was not a rejection of the world per se but a turning toward the true source of one's being. Turning toward God was, for Merton, a returning to the true Self one had always known but had hitherto failed to adequately acknowledge. It was a way of embracing a faith one had always possessed but had hitherto perpetually denied.

In February of 1953, Doubleday published *The Sign of Jonas*—Merton's edited and revised journals from 1946 to 1951. It was the first of Merton's books to be reviewed by the *New York Times*[12] and seemed a far more fitting sequel to *The Seven Storey Mountain* than *Waters of Siloe*—his history of the Cistercians written under assignment from the Abbot. *Sign of Jonas* gave evidence of Merton's concerns as a teacher and signaled a shift from "dogmas as such" to "their repercussions in the life of a soul in which they begin to find a concrete realization."[13]

This very same year, Merton also composed one of his most famous prayers:

> My Lord God, I have no idea where I am going. I do not see the road ahead of me. I cannot know for certain where it will end. Nor do I really know myself, and the fact that I think I am following your will does not mean that I am actually doing so. But I believe that the desire to please you does in fact please you. And I hope that I will never do anything apart from that desire. And I know that if I do this, you will lead me by the right road, though I may know nothing about it. Therefore I will trust you always though I may seem to be lost and in the shadow of death. I will not fear, for you are ever with me, and you will never leave me to face my peril alone.[14]

Clearly Merton's experiences as an educator had taken him into unknown waters and prepared him for yet another spiritual transformation. And yet the great themes of his biography had not changed. He continued to assert that there is a Self deeper than the self we know and a history known only to God *inside* of the history known only to man. To address these hidden realities, one had to speak from some source other than one's goodness or conscience. One had to speak from one's lostness, one's vulnerability, one's trust in God.

The greatest danger to education, Merton believed, was that means and ends were constantly being confused. Even worse, both were forgotten as schools set about producing uneducated graduates, "people unfit for anything except to take part in an elaborate and completely artificial charade which they and their contemporaries have conspired to call 'life'."[15]

He tells the story of the man who was compiling a book on success and had asked him to contribute an essay. Merton wrote back that he had spent the better part of his life strenuously avoiding success and that his best seller was an accident due to inattention and naiveté, and he was taking pains to make sure it would never happen again.

If he had any message to his contemporaries, he wrote, it was this: "Be anything you like, be madmen, drunks, and bastards of every shape and form, but at all costs avoid one thing: success. . . . I believe I can thank Columbia, among so many other things, for having helped me learn the value of unsuccess. . . . Instead of preparing me for one of those splendid jobs (on Madison Avenue) Columbia cured me forever of wanting one. . . . (Mark Van Doren and Joseph Wood Krutch) taught me to imitate not Rockefeller but Thoreau. . . . Life does not have to be regarded as a game in which scores are kept and somebody wins. If you are too intent on winning, you will never enjoy playing. If you are too obsessed with success, you will forget to live. If you have learned only how to be a success, your life has probably been wasted. If a university concentrates on producing successful people, it is lamentably failing in its obligation to society and to the students themselves."[16] Needless to say, Merton's reply was not published, and he never heard from the man again.

CHAPTER SEVEN

TOWARD A POLITICS OF BEING

As the fifties progressed and the number of Merton's publications began to mount, his fame grew, and his correspondence increased. By the end of the decade he was receiving twenty to thirty letters a week and being influenced by a whole new set of writers. Following through on his ecumenical interests, he initiated contacts with a host of international thinkers, most notably Erich Fromm and Czeslaw Milosz.

Fromm's book *Psychoanalysis and Religion* (1950) had allowed Merton to see Christianity as a fundamentally humanistic faith whose chief task was "to enable man to achieve his destiny, to find himself, to be himself: to be the person he was made to become."[1] Fromm's later book *The Sane Society* (1955) had gone on to argue that advanced technological societies dehumanized their populations by frustrating their deepest human needs for love, relatedness, creativity, reason, and ethical responsibility. Neurosis did not come from a failure to conform to the rules of society but from conforming to the rules of a sick society. The more sophisticated the advanced societies became in replacing real human needs with surrogates, simulations, and managed compensations, the more alienated individuals became.

After reading Fromm, Merton came to see that monks had an important role to play in the social ecology of technological civilization as "prophetic exceptions." Their role was to resist conformity in order to give testimony to those human needs and potentials directly under assault by the prevailing social pathologies.

Milosz's book *The Captive Mind* served to temper any facile optimism Merton might have had regarding the possibility of socialist reforms overcoming these problems. Milosz argued that man was not innately good, anymore than nature was better than society. If Pasternak was a "Christian Anarchist" as Merton had once described him, his anarchism, Milosz was quick to point out, had very little to do with the anarchism of Proudhon or the Russian nihilists of the nineteenth century. Fromm was a bit naive to believe you could increase human freedom merely by liberating repressed human desires. One had to become an advocate and witness for the transcendent.

Merton was quick to recognize this call to martyrdom as the true politics of Being. And in "Notes Towards a Philosophy of Solitude," first published in 1955 in the French Journal *Temoignages* under the title "Dans le desert de Dieu,"[2] Merton explored this idea of social liberation predicated upon the attainment of personal integrity. In this essay he invoked Emily Dickinson and Henry David Thoreau as his precursors.

The politics of Being consisted of two stages. The first stressed, like Fromm, the arbitrary nature of social identity and the absurdity of convention—what Henry James once referred to as the "American Joke." At this level, one renounced the fictions of social groups to attain a new sense of unity with all men.

The second stage, exemplified in the work of Eastern European dissidents like Milosz, emphasized that the "throwness" of existence was contained within a larger ontological mystery. "Man's loneliness," Merton wrote, "is, in fact, the loneliness of God. That is why it is such a great thing for man to discover his solitude and learn to live in it. For there he finds that he and God are one: that God is alone as he himself is alone. That God wills to be alone in him. When this is understood, then one sees that his duty is to be faithful to solitude because in this way he is faithful to God."[3]

In other words, our true selves are experienced as a kind of destiny or preternatural force. They are, if you will grant the conceit, "the Christ within" and give testimony to Him in and through our feeling lives. Now the feeling life for a contemplative or a poet is not the same thing as the emotional life. Emotions are the product of sense impressions from without; feelings are interior events evoked by the conscience. Emotions are what we experience when we look at our solitude through the eyes of the world; feelings are what we experience when we look at the world through the eyes of our solitude.

Now if we were to look at American history from the point of view of a "politics of Being," we would see a gradual falling away from spiritual struggle—a slide away from the dialogue between soul and self such as one finds in *Walden*, *Leaves of Grass*, and the poetry of Emily Dickinson to the agitated misery of the existential "outsider" poignantly expressed in the confessions of J. Alfred Prufrock and Holden Caulfield. The story of American letters, in other words, is largely the story of a growing nostalgia for our lost piety as we move further and further away from the contemplative life.

If Whitman and Dickinson were our first and last true ecstatics, then Hemingway represents the last gasp of romantic faith, and our recent Nobel Prize winners Saul Bellow and Toni Morrison provide autopsies of love's body. In between stand the homemade mystics and existential adventurers attempting to cover up the emptiness where the numinous once stood.

But Merton, like his transcendentalist precursors, begins with the premise that "there is in all visible things an invisible fecundity, a dimmed light, a meek namelessness, a hidden wholeness."[4] He doesn't try to arrive there; he *begins* there. When Merton published his pivotal work *No Man Is an Island* in 1955, at the virtual mid-point of his career, he wasn't just offering some interesting spiritual reflections from a cloister—comfortably positioned outside of history. Nor was he merely "taking sides" in the debate over whether God was for or against The Bomb. He was doing something far more profound. He was challenging the prevailing psychology of his day by offering an alternative vision of human nature that began where the existentialists left off, a contemplative vision that moved away from angst and spiritual isolation toward the recognition that all of us participate in the solidarity of solitudes and that this bedrock spiritual reality is the cornerstone upon which any authentic social reform must be built.

No Man Is an Island offered a critique of the American character that directly challenged the popular assumption of an atomist, Protean "self." It explicitly called into question the notions of autonomy advocated by David Riesman in his influential book *The Lonely Crowd* (1950) and spoke in a language all its own of the possibilities that flow from total self-abnegation within the will of God. Its prose was so honest and fresh that it seemed that Merton's life of poverty, chastity, and obedience had given him additional senses capable of penetrating the most elaborate self-justifications and psychological defenses.

"The deep secrecy of my own being," Merton wrote, "is often hidden from me by my own estimate of what I am. My idea of what I am is falsified by my admiration for what I do. And my illusions about myself are bred by contagion from the illusions of other men. We all seek to imitate one another's imagined greatness. If I do not know who I am, it is because I think I am the sort of person everyone around me wants to be. Perhaps I have never asked myself whether I really wanted to become what everybody else seems to want to become. Perhaps if I only realized that I do not admire what everyone seems to admire, I would really begin to live after all. I would be liberated from the painful duty of saying what I really do not think and acting in a way that betrays God's truth and the integrity of my own soul."[5]

Here we see a reflection too complex to be considered "inner directed," "other directed," or "autonomous." Merton is owning up to a deep-seated ambivalence over who he is and what he wants. He does this to resist the bad faith of pretending to know more than he knows. In this sense, Merton's monastic vocation gave him license to postulate fundamental criticisms of conventional life, free from the contentious questioning of motives that plagued secular culture critics. It was as if having given up so many of the joys of ordinary life, he was allowed to be an extremist. Indeed, as a monk in secular America, he was *expected* to be extreme. And once he found the idiom through which to directly express the insights earned by his radical nonconformity, his influence grew by leaps and bounds.

New Seeds of Contemplation and *No Man Is an Island* catapulted Merton back into the center of American intellectual life. These books offered a monastic interpretation of the problems of modernity, arguing that by means of apparent truth and apparent reason, anonymous "principalities of the air" had taken over our lives. Powerful institutions, huge bureaucracies, mass media, and the unseen hand of the market now made up our minds for us in such a way that we were left with the impression that we had done it ourselves. The "revolt of the masses" co-opted by the new "sciences" of advertising and public relations had resulted in a global epidemic of illusion and preening, self-congratulatory deceit.

"One of the few real pleasures left to modern man," Merton lamented, "is this illusion that he is thinking for himself when, in fact, someone else is doing his thinking for him. And this someone else is not a personal authority, the great mind of a genial thinker, it is the mass mind, the general 'they', the anonymous whole. One is left, therefore, not only with the sense that one has thought things out for himself, but that he has also reached the correct answer without difficulty—the answer which is shown to be correct because it is the answer of everybody. Since it is at once my answer and the answer of everybody, how should I resist it?"[6]

Merton believed that in order to overcome this hypnosis of "received ideas" the individual had to assert his or her own personal integrity and leave it to God to restore the unity of the whole. Effective social change did not issue from clever Machiavellian tactics or mass movements but from a refusal by individuals to participate in lies or deceptions. Real change came from what Gandhi called systematic noncooperation with evil by men and women of character and good will.

"He who attempts to act and do things for others or for the world without deepening his own self-understanding, freedom, integrity, and capacity to love," Merton wrote, "will not have anything to give others. He will communicate to them nothing but the contagion of his own obsessions, his aggressiveness, his ego-centered ambitions, his delusions about ends and means, his doctrinaire prejudices and ideas."[7]

Modern civilization had become a production house of illusions. So how does one stop to separate the truth from the half truths, the event from the pseudoevent, reality from the manufactured image?[8] Merton's answer: by following the way of the Desert Fathers. The Desert Fathers knew that individuals not only needed the inspiration of a rigorous religious counterculture *but direct personal contact with a spiritual teacher*. This was the only way one could fully grasp the existential meaning of symbolic communication as an idiom expressing truths not revealed in the official history.

In modern civilization this truth became doubly important because "breakthroughs" in technology had ushered in an age of the sign, where information was replacing wisdom as the content of communication. But through the guru-disciple relationship, one could begin again to grasp "symbols" as evocations of shared inner experiences, and by so doing start the arduous task of building a new civilization within the shell of the old.

If one took a wide enough view of history, monasticism was actually an avant-garde movement, and all the enthusiasm for technological innovation was just a distraction from the real trajectory of history: the on going liberation of the self from oppression and illusion. True individualism, free from petty self-seeking, was not a thing of the past; it was a thing of the future. Our true nature, as persons, has yet to be fathomed, and a culture commensurate with our unique complexities, depths, and sensitivities has yet to exist.

Emily Dickinson knew this, as did Whitman and Thoreau, and all the great anarcho-American humanist progenitors of the politics of Being. Merton's contribution was to establish the ecclesiastical roots of this radically democratic spiritual movement, and by so doing internationalize, historicize, and

Catholicize American Transcendentalism. In his journal from this period he copied out the following quotation from Nikolai Berdyaev: "The very substance of my philosophy is to have nothing at all to do with the thoughts of the times which, so far as I am concerned, are over and done with. I look to the thought of a world which is to begin—the world of a new Middle Ages."[9]

CHAPTER EIGHT

SECOND CALLING

I n 1958 Merton underwent what many have described as a "second conversion" experience. While walking in the shopping district in Louisville, Kentucky, he suddenly saw through the illusion of a separate, holy life apart from the lives of others. According to his own account, standing on the corner, he suddenly experienced a oneness with all the shoppers around him that burst through all the old dualisms separating secular from sacred, monk from world. He realized then that if as a Trappist contemplative he had taken the road less traveled into the soul's undiscovered country, he had not escaped his humanity; he had merely taken the long way home. If his monastic "turn" had made him a "New Man" in Christ, he now saw that that "new man" was an ordinary person, and that the essence of monasticism was not to be found in aloofness from the world but rather in compassion for it and reidentification with it.

"In Louisville, at the corner of Fourth and Walnut, in the center of the shopping district," he wrote, "I was suddenly overwhelmed with the realization that I loved all those people, that they were mine and I theirs, that we could not be alien to one another even though we were total strangers. It was like waking from a dream of separateness, of spurious self-isolation in a special world, the world of renunciation and supposed holiness. The whole illusion of a separate holy existence is a dream. Not that I question the reality of my vocation, or of my monastic life: but the conception of 'separation from the world' that we have in the monastery too easily presents itself as a complete illusion: the illusion that by making vows we become a different species of being, pseudo-angels, 'spiritual men,' men of interior life, what have you. . . . Thank God, thank God that I *am* like other men, that I am only a man among others."[1]

Here Merton exposes the spiritual elitism at the heart of his early books and aphorisms. Monks are not superior to the ordinary person, but through a life devoted to prayer and reflection they can become supremely common, connected, more truly themselves than those of us caught up in worldly illusions dare allow ourselves to be. And, by so doing, through humility, they can come to know others more profoundly than those others know themselves. This does not make monks superior to the average person; only less distracted, and, therefore more real.

For Merton contemporary culture was a collection of disconnected individuals, alienated human beings who had lost their center and extinguished their own inner light. They depended in abject passivity upon the mass in which they cohered without deep feeling or intelligent purpose—functionary cogs in a great economic machine. The vocation of the monk was to construct his own solitude as a first step toward valid encounters with other persons and by so doing show the way—by example—back to essential life.[2]

It was about this time that Merton began reworking his earlier essay "Poetry and Contemplation" to reflect this more prophetic version of monastic responsibility. He revised and republished this essay in October 1958, the very same month that Boris Pasternak won the Nobel Prize for literature. Pasternak had declined the award under pressure from the Soviet Regime, and Merton wanted to defend the essentially mystical message of Pasternak's *Doctor Zhivago* against all the hype threatening to transform it into a mere Cold War political tract.

Pasternak's protagonist, Yuri, the "internal exile," was, for Merton, the model of a twentieth-century Christian apostle. And he wanted to make it clear that Pasternak's novel was a defense of conscience and the interior life, not merely an interpretation of history. In his essay "The Pasternak Affair," Merton compared Pasternak to Dostoyevsky, arguing that the mysticism of Pasternak was more latent, more cosmic, more pagan. For Dostoyevsky, the self-emptying of Christ served as the model for the Christian life. But Pasternak's mysticism was more like Whitman's. It expressed an inclusive sense of God's immanence and omnipresence. "More like the cosmic liturgy of Genesis, than the churchly and hierarchical liturgy of the Apocalypse. What *Zhivago* opposes to Communism," Merton wrote, "is not a defense of Western democracy, not a political platform for some kind of liberalism, and still less a tract in favor of formal religion. *Zhivago* confronts Communism with life itself and leaves us in the presence of inevitable conclusions."[3]

In other words, *Zhivago* dramatizes the power of everyday experience to undermine alienation and expose ideology once it is elevated to the realm of the symbolic though art or religious adoration. Pasternak, Merton tells us, was "a prophet of the original, cosmic revelation: one who saw symbols and figures of the inward, spiritual world, working themselves out in the mystery of the universe around him and above all in the history of men. Not so much in the formal, and illusory, history of states and empires that is written down in books, but in the living transcendental and mysterious history of individual human beings and in the indescribable interweaving of their destinies."[4]

This focus upon the "interweaving of destinies" as opposed to "formal history" underpins the vocations of both the writer and the mystic. Both callings are based upon the recognition of a secret side to life that can only be perceived from an eschatological point of view and described in symbolic or literary terms. The structure of this interior realm is ecological rather than "millennial" because it does not sacrifice the present for some future great event or revolution. Both mystics and writers see the world as a web of relationships, not a hierarchy in time, and they both seek to redeem the moment by "actualizing the eschaton," that is to say, by rendering the present eternal.[5]

On November 10, 1958 Merton wrote a letter to Pope John XXIII proposing for himself a mission as an apostle to the secular world. "I want to tell Your Holiness, as simply as I can," he wrote, "what came to my mind while I was saying Holy Mass yesterday. . . . It seems to me that, as a contemplative, I do not need to lock myself into solitude and lose all contact with the rest of the world; rather this poor world has a right to my solitude."[6] He then goes on to propose setting up a monastic foundation: members would be monks and contemplatives, but at the same time would receive special groups, such as writers, intellectuals, and the like, into their house for retreats and discussions. Although no monastery was ever established, Merton later made trips to California and New Mexico looking for a possible site, and the spirit of dialogue with secular thinkers continued to be one of the driving forces in his life.

Dennis Q. McInerny sees Merton's interest in bridging the sacred and secular worlds as placing him squarely in the heart of what he calls "the Tradition of American Critical Romanticism."[7] This hope in alternative communities is "romantic" to the extent that it is optimistic about what is possible for humankind. But it is also "critical" in that it realizes there are great obstacles standing in the way of human potential. McInerny claims that Merton possessed the "optive mood" in his Christian hope and the critical spirit in his sorrowful recognition of man's unwillingness to respond to God's grace.

McInerny goes on to list six key traits he believes defined American Critical Romanticism: (1) a celebration of individualism; (2) an emphasis upon living life deliberately; (3) an emphasis upon posing a prophetic standard vis-à-vis American culture; (4) a sense of the significance of place; (5) antitechnology; and (6) antigovernment. These six traits are interdependent—valuing the individual person leads to the desire for a life free from illusion and conformity, which leads to a critique of social morality and socioeconomic arrangements, which in turns brings forth a defense of a sense of place and a rejection of governmental and technological intervention. Merton's vision of a secular monastery is the quintessential expression of this tradition.

The only problem here is that McInerny's six traits can be applied to almost every serious American writer since the 1830s. The critical Romantic Tradition *is* the American literary tradition, more or less. The real question is, How does Merton fit into it? In what direction does he qualify it, deepened it, carry it forward?

Merton's chief contribution to contemporary thought may just be his overt refusal to employ conventional political categories in his analysis of cultural phenomena in order to raise political issues to a higher level where spiritual themes enter into dialogue with questions of social ethics. His defense of the contemplative life subverts the grand narratives of both the right- and left-wing political theorists—and directly challenges both the conservative unilinear version of history and the Marxist materialist dialectic. In their place, he offers an eschatological view where progress in the realms of charity, compassion, and gratitude matters more than progress in material prosperity because material progress only feeds the insatiable human desire for more; whereas, an increase in charity and compassion curbs our self-centered inclinations and makes possible the beloved community.

Merton's eschatological vision has inspired a whole generation of spiritual essayists from Wendell Berry and Guy Davenport to Annie Dillard and Henri Nouwen. When I wrote Annie Dillard about Merton's influence on her, she replied: "Sure, I read Merton, and sure, he influenced me enormously. I quoted him in *Pilgrim at Tinker Creek* (I remember a passage, in the last few paragraphs or pages, for one—'itsy bitsy statues') and probably in lots of other places as well—*Holy the Firm, Teaching a Stone to Talk*; I've been steadily reading him for about twenty-five years. And a few years ago I finally took the bait and joined up with the Catholics—something I'm sure I never would have considered if I hadn't read Merton. So sure, he's still in my life, still recommending books. This past summer he recommended Max Picard's *The World of Silence*, from which I derived three poems that will be in the poetry book I am writing. And what writer doesn't think of his prodigious output, and wish he didn't have someone requiring him to write books under obedience?

"The clarity and simplicity of his thought at its best reminds me of Heschel—of any spiritual writer who understands it all so well it becomes simple. His insistence on our adulthood is good—oh, its all good, so very good. The passages about the experience of god and about prayer are of course the key ones for me.

"Somewhere I read recently a wonderfully funny passage— the writer liked Merton only after he forgave him 'the vulgarity of his conversion.' I wish I could refer you to it, but I can't remember where I read it."[8]

One of the consequences of that conversion was that Merton believed that the soul, correctly defined, was not an independent individual essence, but a point of nothingness at the center of our being that belonged entirely to God. And so it was never at our disposal and it was totally inaccessible to reason, the fantasies of our own minds, or the insistence of our own will. One can defend the soul only by acknowledging its transcendent superiority to our private selves and our collective egos. The contemplative's task is simply to see the world from a soul's eye view and then report back, as coherently as he can, what he sees on the far side of history.

In *The Way of Chuang-Tzu*, Merton's translation/interpretation of the great Taoist sage, he equates this soul's eye view with the Tao. The wise man, he tells us, instead of trying to prove some point by logical disputation, sees all things in the light of direct intuition. He is not imprisoned by the limitations of the "I," for the viewpoint of direct intuition is that of both "I" and "not-I." He sees that both sides of every argument have their strengths and weaknesses, and that in the end they are reducible to the same thing once they are related to the "pivot of Tao."

Merton explains, "When the wise man grasps this pivot, he is in the center of the circle, and there he stands while 'yes' and 'no' pursue each other around the circumference."[9] Put simply, the old dichotomies and philosophical antinomies that fuel the dialectic and animate political disputes are simply seen through and thereby abrogated by a more inclusive vision of the whole.

"Religious" social criticism like that embodied in Merton's spiritual reflections challenged the priorities of America's "new class" and suggested a source of legitimization outside those realms dominated by the experts. It addressed a felt sense, not only that the nation needed a creed equal in fervor and resolve to the creed of the communists, but that it needed to find its way back to its own spiritual roots, its own transcendent soul.

Merton believed that we were living through one of the greatest upheavals in human history, but it wasn't the planned revolution of any party or nation state so much as a boiling over of all the inner contradictions that had ever existed. The twentieth century was revealing itself to be a great and solemn revelation of the chaotic forces inside everybody. We had to face it for what it was—a global spiritual crisis. All the inner force of humanity was exploding outward, the good together with the evil. Or as Merton so eloquently described it: "the good poisoned by the evil and fighting it, the evil pretending to be good and revealing itself in the most dreadful crimes, justified and rationalized by the purest and most innocent intentions."[10] In such a world it was the monk's task to defend the common conscience of ordinary people and stand with them against the sophisticated idols of the new Promethean Age.

CHAPTER NINE

PROMETHEUS RECONSIDERED

Between the mid-fifties and the mid-sixties American politics and American letters changed drastically. A large American Left emerged for the first time since the 1930s, and many writers began to embrace political themes. This "new" left emerged, in part, as a legacy of American social criticism of the late forties when postwar culture critics turned from considerations of class injustice to the problems of alienation and cultural malaise.

The Lonely Crowd (1950), *White Collar* (1951), and *The Organization Man* (1956) had all considered the effects of treating other people as things. Each of these books focused on the external versus the internal, the rational versus the emotional, the inauthentic versus the authentic. And part of the popularity of Merton's books, no doubt, came from the fact that they reflected a similar suspicion of "other-directed" conformist values.

However, there was an important difference between these sociological analyses and Merton's religious point of view. For Merton, alienation was a *universal condition*, not a unique sociohistorical development. Everyone in the world was born into the clash between their ambitions and their conscience. You couldn't blame your lack of human solidarity on any particular set of social circumstances, but you could examine *how* particular social circumstances shaped your particular experience of alienation.

Perhaps, the most vivid and useful way of describing Merton's unique analysis of postwar alienation is to contrast his writings to those of Norman Mailer. Mailer's dazzling first novel *The Naked and the Dead* was published the very same year as *The Seven Storey Mountain*, and both books catapulted their authors from obscurity to celebrity overnight. As different as they were in style and subject matter, however, both shared an impatience with modern America's preference for material comfort over nobility of soul. Both also expressed a profound sympathy with the American Adam's desire to start over and reenter the realms of the sacred.

But most significant of all was that both shared the overriding belief that before one could battle the emerging technocracy, one had to withdraw deliberately to the margins of society. The key difference was that Mailer "withdrew" by following the dangerous imperatives of the self in an attempt to dispense with his socially constructed superego. Merton, on the other hand, attempted to transcend the ego altogether through the disciplines of the contemplative life.

As their careers progressed, Mailer set out on a search for a new activist ethic that would "settle for nothing less than making a revolution in the consciousness of our time"— exploring the "wild west of American night life" and charting the new frontiers of violence and sexuality. Merton continued his strategic retreat into the bosom of mother church for character reformation, reeducation, and mystic union.

Merton was suspicious of the illusory "adventureless adventures" of the ego so easily decentered by the shock of the new, preferring instead a desert spirituality that directly confronted the hidden sorrows, lies, and collective grief of the modern wasteland. And unlike Mailer, he did not interpret his experiences in terms of any evolving aesthetic or metaphysic but judged the value of his perceptions entirely by their capacity to unmask illusion. He was, in other words, Norman Mailer's metaphysical antitype: a postmodern ascetic.

Another way of putting this is that Mailer—like many of the novelists of his day—was enamored by complexity and sought out a mastery of the modern. In fact, in *The Naked and the Dead*, one of his characters even says that the only way to escape being a slave to modern institutions is to control them. But since this isn't possible, he rages against despair. In *The Seven Storey Mountain*, Merton locates the institution most extreme in its rejection of modernity—Cistercian monasticism—and serves *that*. Monasticism as a way of life least resembled the life lived in the cities and in the towns. "And there is something in our hearts," Merton noted, "which tells us we cannot be happy in an atmosphere where people are looking for nothing but their own pleasure and advantage and comfort and success."[1]

Mailer embraced all the modern freedoms as assorted avenues into the adventure of self-creation. The new media, the new sexual and social freedoms, the collapsing traditions, opened up realms for self-exploration unknown in former times. Mailer greeted these developments with Nietzschean amor fati—taking them as an opportunity to become a more complex person. Merton, however, did not think that personal genius was a powerful enough countermeasure to meet the depersonalizing forces unleashed by modernity.

"What we need," he insisted, "is the gift of God which makes us able to find in ourselves not just ourselves but Him: and then our nothingness becomes His all. This is not possible without the liberation effected by compunction and humility. It requires not talent, not mere insight, but sorrow, pouring itself out in love and trust."[2] This sorrow pouring itself out in love and trust was Merton's monastic alternative to Mailer's romantic faith in individual creativity.

The modernist literary masters who had most inspired Mailer—Joyce, Dos Passos, Hemingway, and others, had all believed in the virtuoso performance, in the capacity of the single artist to see it all and to see it whole. And if this was no longer literally possible given the growing complexity of the world, then perhaps the mere attempt was in itself instructive—offering us a model of Promethean resolve—however flawed or insufficient. Merton, however, looked to other models of resistance, primarily the example of the Church Fathers who at the height of the Roman Empire retreated into the desert for self-reformation and a direct experience of God. This strategy led them to a very different take on the nature of the self and the meaning of history.

Mailer once remarked that psychology would never come of age until it could explain the psyche of the actor. He was echoing Dostoevsky's view that modern life had largely become a dialectic between the brilliant fraud and pondering naïf. A "psychology of the actor" according to Mailer would examine this dichotomy and, like his essay "The White Negro," reveal the metaphysical longings of common garden-variety American psychopaths.

But in an odd reversal, Thomas Merton's devotional meditations published in the mid-fifties, particularly his spiritual classics *Seeds of Contemplation* and *No Man Is an Island*, fulfill Mailer's aspirations for a new psychology even better than Mailer's own books do because they reveal modern psychology to be the psychology of the actor already. Merton's works point out that we already know the dynamics of the false self; what hasn't been revealed is the psychology of the self who sees through the act! To grasp *that*, one must turn to the literature of the mystics. No, more than that, one must *become* a mystic oneself. Mailer himself must have sensed this—how else to explain his frequent references to mysticism or the apocalyptic revelation at the end of his short story "The Man Who Studied Yoga": "Destroy time and chaos may be ordered"?[3]

David Nobel has written that Mailer began the fifties preaching that "a religious revolution had begun in America, led by the priestly hipsters who were teaching the people to escape their social sinfulness through the grace of sex. But by the end of the 1950's, he had come to the demoralizing conclusion that the high priests of sex were incapable of effecting such a revolution. The forces of darkness were not only entrenched in the institutions and traditions of society, they had infiltrated the inner citadel of the human soul as well. . . . Suddenly, Mailer was no longer concerned with liberating mankind from civilization, but only with the salvation of his own soul."[4]

And so by 1960, Norman Mailer had come round to a tragic skepticism toward the claims of modernity very much like the views Merton held in 1937. The difference was that Mailer continued along the path of the egotistical sublime, embracing defiance, rebellion, and self-assertion rather than asceticism. Mailer, the media warrior/mayoral candidate/controversialist—was a modern Prometheus stealing from heaven the wisdom kept jealously by a struggling, imperfect God. But Thomas Merton saw his task as a writer very differently. For him it was a matter of fulfilling a Christlike destiny as keeper of the divine flame—wrestling from the Pagan God Zeus the creative fire that rightfully belongs to man.

Merton explained this contrast between the Promethean artist and the Christian writer this way: "Prometheus thought he had to ascend into heaven to steal what God had already decreed to give him. But Christ, Who had in Himself all the riches of God and all the poverty of Prometheus, came down with the fire Prometheus needed, hidden in His Heart. And He had Himself put to death next to the thief Prometheus in order to show him that in reality God cannot seek to keep anything good to himself alone."[5]

The Christian writer is not in competition with God for power over the natural world; nor is he God's Gnostic collaborator. He is, rather, drawn to God's light, warmth, and mercy and suffers in his rebellion against the usurper God, Zeus, who would keep him alienated, not only from life but from his own secret, interior, true self. Promethean artists and their Dionysian offspring, like Mailer, try to make secular life transcendent by locating its fire in temporality or sexuality. To do this, they have to go against the stoicism inherent in classical forms by inventing their own mock-heroic tragicomedies.

This is why modernist and postmodernist works are so often "experimental" or sui generis—containing within their structures their own immanent teleologies. Their philosophical assumptions simply preclude the spirituality built into classical forms, and so as a result, they end up focusing on the endless existential ironies and instabilities inherent in a morally chaotic universe. But if one accepts the monastic assumption that there is a providential order unfolding within time and sees traditional religious symbols not as empty tropes discredited by modern science but as forms expressive of actual human feelings carrying with them all the moral and political baggage that makes up the checkered history of Western Christendom, then it becomes possible to testify to human insufficiency and still wait on grace.

Promethean novelists, like Mailer, stand in the no man's land of self-making, conflating fact with fiction (the new journalism!) and fabricating myths and countermyths the way Du Pont fabricates new polymers and plastics. But the significance of their results get muddled. And in Mailer's case, as the exploration gets more and more sordid, the discoveries get less and less clear, until in the end he can do little else but present greater and greater complexities. His artistic detachment turns in upon itself, and we are left with cluttered and circuitous thousand-page novels—comic but souless epics without light whose only value resides in their capacity to register degrees of corruption.

Merton's life as a contemplative placed him in a radically different relationship to his times. Not only did he see through the false claims of modernity (progress, scientific objectivity, the end of ideology) very early, but he spent over twenty years living an alternative, religious existence. As a result, his countercultural views were not based upon any impromptu countermythology or knee-jerk rebellion against the status quo, but upon the spiritual defiance begun by the desert fathers against the Roman super state and purified over time by the contemplatives of Europe. At the heart of his critique of empire resides an entire psychology of moral discernment, and in his celebration of the guru/disciple relationship, a clue as to how we might bring back the sublime to our own ironic age.

In his book *Thoughts in Solitude* (1956) Merton pointed out that sinners had a very keen eye for false virtues and a very exacting idea of what virtue should be in a good man. If in the men who are supposed to be good, sinners see "virtues" that are effectively less vital and less interesting than their own vices, they will conclude that virtue has no value and cling to what they have although they hate it.[6]

Merton was speaking from his own experience here. He too had a keen eye for false virtue and very exacting ideas of what true virtue should be. And he too had used this knowledge to justify himself. In the light of the hypocrisies and failures of others, his sins had seemed quite excusable, vital, interesting: creative necessities. This is one of the reasons, he believed, that so few people aspired to sainthood. It wasn't because anyone believed a life of sin was a good thing. We all know it isn't. But a consistently moral life strikes many of us as unreal, inhuman, perhaps even grandiose. Straightforward corruption seems more honest. As a result of this kind of thinking, modern novelists, like Mailer, flock to psychopaths for clues to the secret dynamics of the élan vital, leaving the saints to bear the burdens of personal authenticity in inglorious silence and public suspicion.

By describing this wager on the side of self-making made by the modern Promethean, Merton allows us to see through the hubris of most modern and postmodern writers. He is not making an argument here, but owning up to what he and the rest of us already suspect: that a part of us really does not want to be virtuous because we fear it will turn us into robots or frauds. That part of us, our "sophisticated," urbanized, secular side, our Protean Self, our "inner Hipster" justifies its false fears, celebrates them, even comes to see them as "principles." No one can be completely honest, so why try? Better an honest fraud than a tiresome, self-deceived, wannabe saint.

Having recognized these sentiments in himself, Merton composed this prayer: "Teach me to bear a humility which shows me, without ceasing, that I am a liar and a fraud and that even though this is so, I have an obligation to strive after truth, to be as true as I can, though I will inevitably find all my truth half-poisoned with deceit. This is the terrible thing about humility: that it is never fully successful. . . . True humility is, in a way, a very real despair: despair of myself, in order that I may hope entirely in You."[7]

Here in a nutshell is Merton's religious antidote to the hubris of "hipsterism" presented in its full psychological difficulty. Here is a hope that is a kind of despair, a paradox of redemption to match the paradox of sin. Unlike Mailer's adventure into the imperatives of the self, it represents a coming home to the even more challenging imperatives of conscience.

"There is a silent self within us," Merton wrote, "whose presence is disturbing precisely because it is so silent: it *can't* be spoken. Now let us frankly face the fact that our culture is one that is geared in many ways to help us evade any need to face this inner, silent self. We live in a state of constant semi-attention to the sound of voices, music, traffic. . . . We are not fully present and not entirely absent; not fully withdrawn, yet not completely available. . . . (But) it is in the depths of conscience that God speaks, and if we refuse to open up inside and look into those depths, we also refuse to confront the invisible God who is present within us. This refusal is a partial admission that we do not want God to be God any more than we want ourselves to be our true selves."[8]

This eloquent analysis of moral evasion is not particularly complicated. Neurosis evolves out of sin, out of our desire to be who we think we should be rather than who we really are. But it is only by conforming to God's truth that we fulfill our true responsibilities, however trivial or banal those responsibilities might appear to our restless, Protean selves who long to transform the consciousness of the age.

Looking back on these two careers, it seems that Mailer has become exhausted by his own worldly success. As the imperatives of his aging, adventurous self weaken, his novels have gotten longer and louder. Mailer chose to engage the world on its own terms, to become a soldier of the night; Merton took a step back through time and the looking glass of modernity to embrace an ecstatic eschatological point of view where the first really were the last and the last really were the first. He looked around at the bop-poetics of Jack Kerouac, the neo-Riechian existentialism of Mailer, and the do-it-yourself mysticism of Henry Miller and saw that the country needed a deeper, spiritual witness.

And although the individualistic rebellion of these writers connected their life stories to the lives of millions of people who were living through the same traumas that they were, Merton knew that more was needed to resist the alienating imperatives of postindustrial society than original ideas. These writers, deprived of any centered life in community and having rejected mass society's substitute gratifications, could find virtue only in improvised living. "The way out," Mailer said, "was the way of the moment." But Merton believed that an authentic *metanoia* or change of heart had to occur, and this change needed to be nourished by continuity with the deep spiritual wisdom of the past. So he entered the sixties with new confidence in his vocation, indeed with a new sense of personal destiny. Every day it was becoming clearer and clearer that the world needed to hear what he had to say.

CHAPTER TEN

THE THIRD POSITION OF INTEGRITY

In 1961 Merton publicly denounced the Cold War as a transparent form of psychological projection and predicted that liberal support for the early Civil Rights Movement would prove too thin—ultimately leading to a conservative backlash and retreat to ethnic nationalisms. As a result of such remarks, he found himself identified with the New Left.

But Merton was uncomfortable with these associations and in a letter to Czeslaw Milosz protested: "It seems to me, as you point out, and as other writers like yourself say or imply (Koestler, Camus, etc.) there has to be a third position, a position of integrity, which refuses subjection to the pressures of the two massive groups arranged against each other in the world. It is quite simply obvious that the future, in plain dialectical terms, rests with those of us who risk our heads and our necks and everything in the difficult, fantastic job of finding out the new position, the ever changing and moving 'line' that is no line at all because it cannot be traced out by political dogmatists."[1]

For the next several years, Merton tried to describe this moving line in a series of books on spiritual discernment: *Wisdom in the Desert*, *Spiritual Direction and Meditation*, and a collection of essays on social and religious issues, *Disputed Questions*. Each of these books in their own unique ways attempted to articulate a spiritual alternative to the political vision of man offered by Gog and Magog—Merton's name for the twin titans vying for victory in the Cold War. The imagery here—taken from the prophecy of Ezekiel—was not meant to equate the morality of the West with that of the Soviet Bloc, but rather to reveal the presence in our midst of two powerful, unholy forces battling over territory and influence. Meanwhile the true God of history continued quietly to guide his people silently along the narrow ridge between moral acquiescence and self-destruction.

In a series of essays, later published under the title "Inner Experience," Merton tried to describe what it was like living on that ridge. His thesis—deftly articulated by William J. Shannon in his book *Thomas Merton's Dark Path* (Farrar, Straus, Giroux 1981)—was that a monk's true subjectivity, his interior I, had no projects: it sought to accomplish nothing, not even contemplation. It sought only to *be* and to move according to the secret dynamics of being itself, following, not its own desires, but the promptings of a "superior Freedom." This superior freedom was the sense of emotional fulfillment that comes from doing the will of God in the moment by being present to His presence. At first glance this may not seem like a third "political" position at all, but it begins to describe the dynamics of that "moving line" that constitutes a life lived in accord with conscience.

Merton put it this way: "The task of the solitary person and the hermit is to realize within himself, in a very special way, a universal consciousness and to contribute this, to feed this back insofar as he can, into the communal consciousness which is necessarily more involved in localized consciousness, and in such a way that there is a dialectical development toward a more universal consciousness."[2] By seeking purity of heart in himself, the dissident monk prepares the way for an authentic universal consciousness. And as we have seen, purity of heart requires "not talent, not mere insight, but sorrow, pouring itself out in love and trust."[3]

The shallow 'I' of individualism can be possessed, developed, cultivated, and pandered to because it is the center of all our striving for gain and satisfaction. But the deep 'I' of the spirit, of solitude and of love cannot be 'had,' possessed, developed, or perfected. It can only be, and act according to the inner laws which are not of man's contriving but which come from God. These Laws of the Spirit are like the wind; they blow where He wills.

Merton comments, "This inner 'I', who is always alone, is always universal; for in this inmost 'I' my own solitude meets the solitude of every other man and the solitude of God."[4] This solidarity of solitudes is the only foundation upon which a critique of contemporary society can be based. The common good, in other words, is not a project to be completed, but an ever-present reality to be discovered, faced up to, affirmed, and won back. It is a call to responsibility in the moment through a recognition of our obligations to the deeper self within us.

With the publication of these books on spiritual discernment, Merton's writings shifted from an otherworldly rejection of secular society's false confidence in material progress to a focus upon prophetic witness as the sine qua non of meaningful social change. In a series of trenchant analyses of public issues that followed the publication of "Inner Experience," Merton established himself as a visionary social critic, a theologian of change, and an advocate of Christian hope as an antidote to modern existential despair. He did this, however, not by replacing the unconscious politicization of the American status quo with an explicit politicization along more egalitarian lines. This was the strategy of the old left. Rather he sought an explicit depoliticization of institutions as a step toward true egalitarianism.

This could only be accomplished, he believed, through a reconsideration of the nature of politics itself. Gandhi and the Desert Fathers had shown him the way: one protested best by living an alternative life. But not just any alternative life: if the monastic reformer/saint/revolutionary demonstrated the slightest trace of self-interest, violence, fear, or self-seeking, he played into the hands of the enemies of God and therefore the enemies of both plebeian life and social reform. But if he could somehow find the courage and the resolve to stand up for the truth unfolding within him, then progressive reforms would follow inevitably—albeit in unpredictable ways.

This was the great Gandhian insight. Nonviolence is not centered upon a faith in one's own particular cause but upon a faith in the truth, which transcends one's own aspirations. The nonviolent soldier of truth does not believe he will always win, nor even that he is necessarily right, only that the truth is so precious that it is worth seeking regardless of the immediate consequences to oneself, and so we must act on what we know, and do, what our conscience is telling us must be done. In other words, nonviolence is a refusal to live a lie or tolerate evil, not because we are more moral than our adversaries but because we have become convinced that only the truth can set us free.

Nonviolence is the political dimension of the monk's quest for purity of heart, and as such it constitutes a Pascalian wager on the side of mankind's traditional, if unfounded, ontological predisposition. It is a form of therapeutic action that attempts to break out of the enchanted enclosure of modern consciousness to challenge history itself as the inescapable pre-category to all human thought. Nonviolent noncooperation with unjust laws is, like monasticism itself, a search for transhistorical absolutes. It is a way of life, not a tactic for change.

Martin Luther King once had all his volunteers sign a commitment card that read, in part, "REMEMBER always the nonviolent movement in Birmingham seeks justice and reconciliation—not victory."[5] By setting justice and reconciliation above political success, King linked the struggle for civil rights to the religious dissident's search for truth. As a result, his protests became a means for demystifying the prevailing unjust politicization of the African American experience, not just another power grab.

This willingness to submit to a truth higher than one's own aims gave the early civil rights movement its radical energy and moral stature. Its goals were not simply to desegregate the buses in Montgomery or the lunch counters in Louisville, but to alter the moral character of the nation by seeking to live in conformity with the superior freedom of God. As a result of this fervor for the truth, the early civil rights movement came to represent for Merton the closest thing he had yet seen to a living expression of the "third position of integrity." Like the monastic movement, it required from its disciples a lifelong commitment to the disinterested pursuit of the good and a willingness to enter a dark night of struggle so that they—and their enemies—might be born again: purged of demeaning social stereotypes and liberated from self-aggrandizing illusions.

The fact that the majority of modern Americans doubted the sincerity of such sublime goals made Merton skeptical of the success of secular political reforms, but at the same time it also convinced him of the importance of nonviolence as a way of life, ecumenicalism as a guiding principle, and dialogue as the necessary first step toward world peace. Merton's own particular contribution to the social movements of the late fifties and early sixties was to call attention to the ethical implications of nonviolence and to point out misapplications of Gandhian principles. Because of this, he was sometimes seen as the spiritual conscience of the New Left, a kind of "believing beatnik." But he saw his role differently. By exposing the inability of all contending parties to respond to the radical, religious dimension of Gandhi's truth, Merton was pointing the way toward a suprapolitical activism keyed not to any ideological principles but to the mysterious will of God unfolding within the lives of individual souls struggling to regain their conscience.

In 1960 Merton wrote a letter to Dorothy Day after she had been arrested several times for refusing to participate in air-raid drills. "I am deeply touched by your witness to peace," he wrote. "I see no other way, though of course the angles of the problem are not all clear. I am certainly with you on taking some kind of stand and acting accordingly. Nowadays it is no longer a question of who is right but who is at least not a criminal—if any of us can say that anymore. So don't worry about whether or not in every point you are perfectly all right according to everybody's book; you are right before God as far as you can go and you are fighting for a truth that is clear enough and important enough. What more can anybody do?"[6]

It is tempting to read this remark as a symptom of political frustration, but it is more truly an expression of Merton's recognition of the limits inherent in any act of social protest. Our responsibility as citizens is to follow our conscience even though we do not know exactly where it is leading us, and even though others tell us that we are wrong. Politics is an intractable tangle of good and evil motives, but we will never untie the knot if we lose hope.[7] Finding the good was, for Merton, the ongoing task of spiritual discernment.

"There is much to be learned," he wrote. "Peace is to be preached, non-violence is to be explained as a practical method, and not left to be mocked as an outlet for crackpots who want to make a show of themselves. Prayer and sacrifice must be used as the most effective spiritual weapons in the war against war, and like all weapons, they must be used with deliberate aim: not just with a vague aspiration for peace and security, but against violence and war."[8]

Merton's mission had taken a political turn, fostered by his perception of himself as a "guilty bystander." In his "Letter to a White Liberal," published in 1961, he was particularly hard on those whites who supported the civil rights movement only in order to protect "a certain image of themselves." He felt their commitment was shallow and warned that they could not be counted on to follow through with a real democratization of national priorities, and that the result of this failure would be even greater domestic discord. Legal reforms, however well meaning, would never heal the racial problems in this country if they were based upon some brokered compromise.

Once again, Merton was asserting the monastic imperative of purity of intention over worldly success. Knowing the good to be willed was more important that willing the good. Reforms built upon half-truths never last, and a pseudo Black identity born of liberal concessions was a recipe for disaster. Only an authentic identity forged by African Americans themselves, on their own terms, in open, unfettered dialogue with God almighty and his inscrutable will in history could free the Negro from the bondage of second-class citizenship.

And yet Merton insisted that the Negro "problem" was really a White problem. Segregation was rooted in the White man's racial identity—not the Black's.[9] Martin Luther King had offered Whites a way out. Rather than see the problem as a question of Black against White, they could join him in recognizing it as a clash between Good and Evil, nonviolent Justice against violent Injustice. But White America did not seize the opportunity to join in solidarity with their prophetic Black brother, and the moment for national healing was lost. King's movement fragmented into schisms, and we all now had to take the long walk home through the difficult terrain of competing ethnic nationalisms and political "solutions."

These views of Merton's were sharply criticized at the time by Martin Marty as the cheap shots of a cloistered choir boy removed from the difficult problems of race relations in the city. But after the long hot summer of 1967, Marty apologized to Merton in an open letter in the *National Catholic Reporter*.[10] It wasn't Merton's profound grasp of sociological dynamics that had led to his accurate forecast. What made his "Letter to a White Liberal" so prophetic was his religious insight that the Cold War and the civil rights movement were actually two sides of the same coin—two different ways of addressing the same ongoing search for national identity and purpose.

The responsibility of a religious social critic is not to tell the oppressed they are oppressed (they know that), but to tell those who think they are "free" that they are really oppressed. In fact, this was precisely Merton's message to White America: you are not free. You are deaf to the call of the living God of history speaking through his Black messengers, and the price you must now pay for refusing their call is to forfeit their wisdom. You must now watch as Black brothers of good will turn their backs on your society, for you have lost your opportunity to liberate the country from all the mythologies of race that were, as W. E. B. Dubois had observed, making the twentieth century the century of the color line.

In 1962 Merton wrote a letter to James Forest that stands at the heart of his social critique: "It seems to me of course that the most basic problem is not political, it is a-political and human. One of the most important things to do is to keep cutting deliberately through political lines and barriers and emphasizing the fact that these are largely fabrications and that there is another dimension, a genuine reality, totally opposed to the fictions of politics, the human dimension which politicians pretend to abrogate entirely to themselves. Is this possible? I am accused of being too ready to doubt the possibility, though I am as ready as anyone to put some hope in it. At least we must try to hope in that; otherwise, all is over. But politics as they now stand are hopeless. Hence the desirability of a manifestly non-political witness, non-aligned, non-labeled, fighting for the reality of man and his rights and needs in the nuclear world in some measure against all the alignments."[11]

This strategy of continually "cutting across political lines and barriers" was perhaps the most telling innovation introduced into American politics by King's application of Gandhian civil disobedience. What made the grassroots movements of the late fifties and early sixties so inspiring was precisely their suprapolitical politics; their capacity to inspire by their unconventional, idealistic-moral-religious take on matters so conventionalized most people had simply ceased to see them as containing any potential for change—such as the relations between the races, the role of women in society, and the ends of higher education. But as this grassroots "rebellion" became formalized and factored into the contending ideological alignments, it lost its inclusive thrust and dissolved into various strains of an "adversary culture" defined more by what it opposed than by what it affirmed.

Merton's book of poems *Emblems of a Season of Fury*, published in 1963 (perhaps his best poetry collection), attempted to expose the fictions of politics and to blow the lid off conventional views of the relationship between religion and morality. He addressed topics as varied as the deaths of Ernest Hemingway and James Thurber, the Moslems' Angel of Death, Asia, Rome, the Children of Birmingham, the Holocaust, Love, Chartres Cathedral, feminine spirituality, and the Soviet threat. The collection challenged readers to shift gears and broaden their perspectives. Each poem seemed to demand a whole new order of attention and focus.

This was a deliberate strategy, a no-holds-barred attempt to cut across all political lines and barriers. Merton believed that it was vitally important to keeping the way wide open for thought and discussion. In a letter to Ping Ferry, vice president of the Center for the Study of Democratic Institutions in Santa Barbara, Merton warned against "getting oneself permanently identified and so to speak classified as the holder of one or another set of opinions. And by implication, as loyal or disloyal to our side of the cold war. Even to question the primary importance of this kind of loyalty is itself regarded as disloyalty and immediately disqualifies all that one says from further consideration. We have got to keep thinking and asking questions. And the mere ability, once in a while, to raise the right question ought to be regarded as an achievement. May we learn to do this and keep at it. What did the Fathers of the Church say about Socrates being among the saints? And then there are also the Prophets."[12]

Merton's own method for probing different perspectives was to inhabit them. In one of his most celebrated poems, "Chant to Be Used in Processions Around a Site with Furnaces"—he explores in the first person singular the point of view of a concentration camp commandant. The narrator describes his work as an executioner, how the children were pacified, repeating the refrain, "I made improvements!"[13] Merton dramatizes unthinking acquiescence to evil—bringing to language the self-justifications used by those who would carry forward the "philosophy" of the apparatchiks.

Looking at the poem closely, we can see all the qualities of the authoritarian personality. its selfless dedication to the task at hand. Its focus on practical improvements, innovations, progress. Its refusal to be detracted by sentiment or the claims of conscience. Its attention to detail at the expense of the big picture. Pride in personal achievements. Obedience to immediate superiors. The poem does not oppose this "perspective" but rather through sympathetic magic exorcises *our sense of distance and superiority from it.* "Do not think yourself better," its last lines warn, "because you burn up friends and enemies with long range missiles without ever seeing what you have done."[14]

In his "Original Child Bomb: Points for Meditation to be Scratched on the Walls of a Cave," Merton employs a similar rhetorical strategy. Only in this poem he is not dramatizing the self-justifications of a Nazi commandant but the denatured language of the expert and professional. Even today it is chilling to read.

The poem is a straightforward account of the events leading up to and following the bombings of Hiroshima and Nagasaki designed, in minimalist fashion, to evoke the "logic" animating the impersonal efficiency of modern warfare. Military scientists and engineers as it turns out used words and phrases from Christian mythology and their own private lives as code names for the mission. When the bomb was successfully tested in New Mexico, Churchill received the coded announcement: "Babies satisfactorily born." "Trinity" was the name given the first test blast. "Little Boy" was the name of the bomb dropped on Hiroshima. "Papacy" was the name given to the landing location of the plane. "Enola Gay," the name of Col. Tibbets's mother in Iowa, was the name given the plane carrying the bomb. Merton notes that Tibbets was a "well-balanced" man who did not have a nervous breakdown after the bombing like some of the other members of his crew.

Merton discovered that by juxtaposing the language of military intelligence with its campy arch symbolism against the horrific realities they described, he could dramatize the death of the symbol in the birth of the sign. Secret codes had replaced ancient mythologies, and clandestine elites were now in control of weapons of mass destruction. The totalitarian age was upon us even in victory. World War II had been a plague so virulent that even those attempting to eradicate power-mad regimes began to manifest, in their own defense of humanity, traits not unlike their enemies. To establish killing as a rational policy, the language of the experts was used to disguise and justify horrendous deeds. Merton believed it was his task to expose this false rhetoric and the new class of bureacrats and experts who were benefiting from it.

This frontal assault upon the erzsat postivism of the postwar culture was a decidedly different tack than that taken by most Christian activists of the day. Niebuhr, for example, not only believed that in a fallen world it was necessary for the "new class" of experts to flex their political muscle, but he made it his calling to explain exactly how that muscle ought to be flexed. The "Christian Realist" had to make tragic calculations and to render unto Caesar what was Caesar's, so that he could render unto God that which was God's. But Merton held to the possibility, as did Gandhi and Martin Luther King, Jr., that moral compromise may not be quite as endemic as it seems to practicing politicians. Instead of measured policy recommendations, he sought to discover a truly universal ethic. And he wagered his entire life on the possibility that he might be able to find one. Indeed the quest for purity of heart, upon which the monk wagered the salvation of his everlasting soul, demanded of him nothing less.

CHAPTER ELEVEN

THE MYSTIC AS PUBLIC INTELLECTUAL

W e hear a lot these days about the need for intellectuals
to address public policy issues, calls for the end to
professional jargons in the humanities and for the rebirth of democratic dialogue enlivened and nuanced by professional critics, historians, and philosophers. But so far these
calls have largely brought forth only Naomi Wolfs, Rush Lim-
baughs, Susan Faludis, and Dinesh D'Souzas—spokespersons
for various causes with their publicity kits in one hand, their
best-sellers in the other, and their opinions on their sleeve.
Driven by the star system to increasingly inflate their intellectual product line and to identify ever more rigidly with some
easily identifiable constituency, such figures lose in subtlety
whatever they gain in notoriety and end up producing one shrill
manifesto after another. As their ideas thin, their accessibility
increases, and so their popularity grows even larger, until
whole "movements" are mobilized around study groups, think
tanks, and weekend retreats. Witness the current proliferation
of the best-selling "virtue" books specifically marketed to children, teens, young adults, even seniors. Not to mention the recent spate of nonbooks published by academic presses under
the rubric "cultural studies" that are merely collections of pa-
pers and speeches delivered at various conferences on popular
topics. What is wrong about all this is that the ideas dissemi-
nated are invariably superficial given their author's aspirations
for immediate and tangible success.

Thomas Merton represents the very antithesis to this trend. Although he became famous with his first book, perhaps even the most famous monk in American history, he did not exploit his celebrity. On the contrary, he immediately published a series of rather esoteric Trappist tracts and didn't even leave the monastery grounds for ten years. When he reemerged into public life in the late fifties, it was as a committed advocate of monasticism. And when he joined in the public debates in the early sixties over the Cold War and Civil Rights, it was to defend the spiritual roots of democracy against what he saw as the twin evils of bureaucracy and militarism. By simply remaining true to his vows, Merton had become—by no plan of his own—the very epitome of the community-based intellectual who practiced what he preached. Through him, monasticism once again became a sign of hope and a sign of protest.

In 1964 Merton held a retreat at Gethsemani for leaders in the Peace Movement: Daniel and Philip Berrigan, Jim Forest, Wilbur H. Ferry, A. J. Muste, John Howard Yoder, John Nelson, Tom Cornell, and Tony Walsh. They discussed the spiritual roots of social protest, and in November of that same year Merton published "Gandhi: The Gentler Revolutionary" in *Ramparts Magazine*. Merton was fifty years old by then and self-consciously addressing the same questions that his mentor Aldous Huxley had raised in his book *Ends and Means* back in 1936: "How can the regression in charity be halted and reversed? How can the existing society be transformed into the ideal society described by the prophets? How can the average sensual man and the exceptional (but more dangerous) ambitious man be transformed into those non-attached beings, who alone can create a society significantly better than our own?"[1]

Merton's strategy, following the lead of St. Benedict, was to shift the terms of the debate by addressing these questions at the community level. Suddenly what seem like impossibly abstract issues became grounded in the dynamics of community life—particularized, historicized, and psychologized. Most "public intellectuals" speak to issues addressing our public selves and so they usually consider only the most superficial, nonbinding, sociological aspects of existence. On the other hand, private thinkers address issues of personal fulfillment, ignoring the larger social ramifications. But at the community level our concerns as individuals trying to get along with one another are brought to the foreground. This is the level where nonviolence has its most lasting impact. And it was at this level that Merton focused his Trappist critique of American culture.

American society was tainted, Merton believed, by the inauthenticity, unconscious dissimulation, and inflated personalities of its leaders as much as it was by the inefficiencies of its laws and institutions.[2] And so if we were serious about social reform, we had better begin at the community level with the reformation of our own lives—fighting the fascist within as well as the fascist from without.

Merton worried about all the attention directed toward him and about his capacity to make the case for the contemplative life given his increasing fame and influence. He wrote in his journal: "What a weary, silly mess. When will I learn to go without leaving footsteps? A long way from that: I still love recognition and need to preach, so that I will believe in my own message and believing that, will believe in myself—or at least consent to find myself acceptable for a while. Absurdity, and very dishonest on top of it. I wish I knew how to be otherwise! Funny how I came to this, quite in spite of myself and in spite of everything, after several days of desperation (half-felt) and perplexity. Peace in seeing the hills, the blue sky, the afternoon sun. Just this and nothing more! As soon as I move toward anything else, confusion. Those asses and their active philosophy and their itch to go on any stupid bandwagon! Yet how I am influenced by them in spite of myself! They are so sure that is Christianity—that parading and gesticulating, that proclamation of ten thousand programs!"[3]

Merton agreed with the New Left that the prevailing technological society had given itself over to one-dimensional values, and that the old institutional structures were simply not in a position to overcome this reification of Being having themselves profited by it. But the emerging counterculture—impressed by its ability to see through the old order—did not sufficiently acknowledge its own psychological dependency upon the powers that be. And so, paradoxically, the more accurately it analyzed the failures of the "system," the more it exacerbated its problems by polarizing the country and refusing to recognize its role in perpetuating the impasse.

Again, Merton turned to the Old Testament prophets, the Desert Fathers, and the Zen masters for models of more effective ways of speaking truth to power. "Today more than ever," he wrote, "we need to recognize that the gift of solitude is not ordered to the acquisition of strange contemplative powers, but first of all to the recovery of one's deep self, and to the renewal of an authenticity which is twisted out of shape by the pretentious routines of a disordered togetherness. What the world asks of the priest today is that he should be first of all a *person* who can give himself because he has a self to give. And, indeed, we cannot give Christ if we have not found him, and we cannot find him if we cannot find ourselves."[4]

As the Vietnam War expanded and the country began to split at the seams, Merton continued to pursue the political and ecumenical interests he had begun at the start of the decade. His dialogue with the East deepened, his take on nonviolence entered a new phase, and he moved into his own private hermitage on the grounds of Gethsemani.

On January 22, 1965, he noted in his journal a projection made in the *Kiplinger Investment Newsletter* for the year 1980. Kiplinger had predicted no world war, just more of everything: more highways, more schools, more suburbs, more money, more fun, even more music, art, and literature. Though Kiplinger did not say, Merton notes, whether or not there would be more jobs.

"What a total lack of imagination!" Merton wrote in his journal. "The prophecy is unimaginative enough to be perhaps even *true*, but how intolerable. Nothing to look forward to but the same inanities, falsities, clichés, and pretenses. But there will surely be more frustration, therefore more madness, violence, degeneracy, addiction. The country will be one vast asylum."

Then he goes on to write: "I have higher hopes. I dare to hope for *change*, not only quantitative but qualitative too; such change must come through darkness and crisis, not joyous painless adventure. Perhaps, I say that out of habit."[5] In February 1965, Merton made his first public protest of the war in Vietnam in a letter to *Commonweal*, and in August 1965 he obtained permission from his abbot to live the life of a hermit full time. He was writing at a furious pace now on a variety of themes and concerns. His essays were being published in a variety of popular journals—and his following, both in and out of the church, was getting very large.

The autobiographical sermon begun in *The Seven Storey Mountain* had all but dissolved itself into a series of observations and conversations with other thinkers and traditions. And with these dialogues came darker insights into the meanness of conventional life, the unthinking immorality of the social systems within which we operate, and the false triumphalism of the church hierarchy. No one could accuse Merton now of being a simple Catholic apologist; he was a man of faith in thoughtful conversation with a faithless age.

At the very moment he was retreating even further into solitude, he began writing more directly to and about the world. His writing was becoming more and more political as he was beginning to see how tainted the public discourse had become, how insufferable were the sacrifices the young were being asked to make to a false conception of national pride, and how misguided was the "Death of God" Theologians' sunny response to the triumph of modernity—"betraying man's inner spirit and turning him over like Samson, with his hair cut off and his eyes dug out, to turn the mill of a self-frustrating and self-destroying culture."[6]

While many others protested the Vietnam War as a peculiar instance of postmodern dehumanization demanding across-the-board reform of every existing American institution, Merton refused to see it as uniquely evil and instead protested *all wars*. He sought, in other words, to expose the *universal ground* of the conflict, rather than "historicize" it. Gandhi didn't provide historical critiques of particular constitutional injustices but directly confronted injustice through acts of high conscience. This was quite different from the ideological criticism that actually emptied specific events of their moral significance by recasting them as examples of larger historical dynamics requiring "strategic responses" rather than personal sacrifice.

Merton published *Conjectures of a Guilty Bystander* in 1966 as a sequel to *The Sign of Jonas*. He described it as a "confrontation of twentieth-century questions in light of the monastic commitment" and as a series of "sketches and meditations, some poetic and literary, others historical and even theological, fitted together in a spontaneous, informal philosophic scheme in such a way that they react upon each other. The total result was a personal and monastic meditation, a testimony of Christian reflection in the mid-twentieth century."[7]

With the publication of this work, Merton became a creature of dialogue, a "worker" in the realms of the spirit, rather than an ethereal voice whispering profundities through a crack in the monastery wall. At this time in his life, his reading, which had always been eclectic and extensive, became even more varied. He studied the works of Protestant theologians such as Karl Barth, Dietrich Bonhoeffer, and Paul Tillich, and the works of such radical social theorists as Herbert Marcuse, Mary Daly, Ivan Illich, and Roland Barthes. He even reread his old favorites William Faulkner, Aeschylus, and Albert Camus.

It was also at this time that the church censored Merton's antiwar articles. So he self-published them anyway in a series of circulars and mimeographed letters. By the middle of the 1960s Merton's poetry was being quoted by Lenny Bruce in his nightclub act, and Eldridge Cleaver even mentioned him in *Soul on Ice*. "Despite my rejection of Merton's theistic world view," Cleaver wrote, "I could not keep him out of the room. He shouldered his way through the door. Welcome, Brother Merton. I give him a bear hug. Most impressive to me was Merton's description of New York's black ghetto—Harlem. I liked it so much I copied out the heart of it in longhand. Later, after getting out of solitary, I used to keep this passage in mind when delivering Black Muslim lectures to other prisoners."[8]

Again Merton protested in a letter to Czeslaw Milosz, "I am not identified with the young American subsociety. I give them my sympathy, but like you I stop at the business of hating for hating's sake what is so transparently easily hated. . . . And as to Zen, well, it might just turn out that my Zen had nothing to do with theirs."[9]

It is not hard to understand what led to Merton's increasing misgivings about the counterculture. Certainly his correspondence with Milosz had tempered his enthusiasm for socialism as a "solution." And although he understood, even predicted, the Black Revolution's move away from nonviolence, he never approved of it. Merton had also been taken aback by Aldous Huxley's advocacy of LSD, and wrote him a letter asking him how he could have attributed a "mystical" experience to a drug, given that in mystical prayer God must be given the freedom *not to respond*; whereas, a drug *must* respond. LSD was just a one-sided manipulation.

When Roger La Porte, a Catholic peace activist, set himself on fire and died protesting the Vietnam War on November 9, 1965, Merton temporally quit the Fellowship of Reconciliation, a Catholic Peace Organization. Although he was dedicated to abolishing war and preserving the dignity of the individual soul, he was, unlike Dorothy Day or the Berrigans, not at all sure that the best way to accomplish this was by building a mass movement. The atrocities of the Russian Revolution, Mao's Cultural Revolution, and the Nazi Plague warned him against simple enthusiasm for movements celebrating the people or announcing the need for revolutionary reforms. One's aspirations for sainthood, he knew quite well, were not enough to insure the morality of one's deeds. Before one could *will* the good, first one had to know what the good *was*. Good intentions were always suspect; *purity* of intention was everything.

I bring this up not to impeach Dorothy Day's status as an authentic Christian hero—I believe she is one—but rather to distinguish her views from those of Merton's. Like her, Merton brought Christian values to bear on public policy and advocated nonviolence, voluntary poverty, a life of service, and solidarity with the poor. But whereas Dorothy Day kept her ideological balance all her life, living and dying a Christian socialist, Merton's politics were never so clearly defined.

Although he was an advocate of Gandhian noncooperation with evil, he was not optimistic about secular reform movements. He believed in original sin, in the intoxication of power, and in the amnesia of the masses, and so he placed his hope not upon the natural man but on the divine light. This put him into tension with certain elements within the Christian Left who embraced the need for secular revolution as the sine qua non of cultural reformation.

Late in 1965, Merton began counseling draft resisters and wrote an essay on Bob Dylan as the "American Villon." The counseling put him under surveillance by the FBI, but he was by no means antigovernment. "The problem," Merton explained, "is to learn how to renounce resentment without selling out to the organization people who want everyone to accept absurdity and moral anarchy in a spirit of uplift and willing complicity."[10] Draft resisters were men following their conscience and so deserved to be supported. But Merton was not calling for mass resistance, he was still struggling to find some third position of integrity vis-à-vis the conflicts tearing the country in two.

In 1966, after many years of seemingly fruitless struggle against the war in Vietnam, Jim Forest, feeling burnt out, wrote to Merton asking for advice. Merton replied: "Do not depend upon the hope of results. When you are doing the sort of work you have taken on . . . you may have to face the fact that your work will be apparently worthless and achieve no result at all, if not perhaps results opposite of what you expect. As you get used to this idea you start more and more to concentrate not on the results but on the value, the rightness, the truth of the work itself."[11]

Here Merton is advising Forest to take the long view of things; he is cautioning him against falling into bitterness and resentment at the failure of his own idealism. He is counseling him to adopt the long-suffering, eschatological perspective of the monk, a perspective in which everyday life is a form of dissent and the alternative of God's Kingdom is ever present, right before one's eyes. That is to say, he is telling him to live in the truth of the final judgment now, whatever the seeming costs, whatever the immediate difficulties or sacrifices.

Not that Merton himself found this an easy thing to do. Shortly after this letter was written, Merton began a fleeting romance with a student nurse he met while in the hospital for back surgery. The fullest description of this relationship can be found in Michael Mott's biography *The Seven Mountains of Thomas Merton.*[12] It turns out that they were alone together several times, and that is about as explicit as the record gets. The "affair" had all the markings of romantic infatuation—love letters, poems, late-night phone calls—but from the start it was an impossible match.

The relationship tormented Merton and deepened his sense of solitude. He wanted to continue seeing her, and yet he knew he couldn't. Their contacts became fewer as the year progressed, with no communication at all toward the end of 1967. He called her one last time in 1968, six months before he died, but by then they had already grown very far apart.

There is a temptation to make more of this than it deserves, to see it as Merton's nod in the direction of the sexual revolution and his "liberation" into physical, human love. But it is important to remember that by contemporary standards this was a very innocent liaison, and unlike the other celebrated monk/poet from the sixties, William Everson (aka Brother Antoninus), Merton never left his order. Indeed Everson not only left his order, he got married and went on to write a whole cycle of erotic love poems describing his new way of life. Merton was more like Kafka, who after calling off one of his engagements, remarked: "I couldn't do it. To marry her would have been to deny the nothingness that I have become."

The entire experience actually deepened Merton's commitment to his holy vows. He knew now in a very intimate way that there were forces at play upon his life and psyche that were quite simply beyond his control, and so the wisest action was to accept the limitations imposed upon him by the teaching authority of the church—not because he necessarily agreed with the reasons his superiors professed for limiting his love life "but out of love for God who is using these things to attain ends which I myself cannot at the moment see or comprehend."[13]

It was about this time that some of Merton's activist friends began pressuring him to leave the monastery and join the antiwar movement full time. He responded with his typical insistence on the need for personal authenticity: "The only place you can stop the war in Vietnam is to be where you belong, where God wants you to be. If you're in the wrong place, there's nothing you can do. If I give up where God wants me to be, I can do nothing. Its just a question of being where I'm supposed to be. Not where I want to be."[14]

He admitted that many of the people he was in tune with—artists, philosophers, scientists—were outside the church. But he found that the so-called progressive voices, Christians among them, were still more or less just Great Society Liberals. "They have an optimism," he wrote, "that basically accepts the status quo, and they are not all that different from those who are fearful. They offer some good insights and new images, but for the most part, they're happy, not alienated, and think our society is good and really going somewhere. What they say is useless. In reality, they see no alternative."[15]

The problem with political thinkers of both the left and the right is that they truly believe they know what needs to be done and so set about doing it. This impiety, from Merton's contemplative point of view, was the essence of original sin. Such "activists" had eaten from the tree of the knowledge of good and evil, and so they now knew who was naked and who was to blame and who had to be sacrificed. This is why Merton believed that the best hope for secular reform came from people inside the church who distrusted their own theoretical acumen as a point of doctrine. Monasticism, as a set of ascetic practices, was specifically designed to undermine intellectual pride. And so it offered a way of protest built upon a recognition of God's presence in the world as it now stood, rather than calling for a sacrifice of the present to the future.

Merton's letters to and from Rosemary Radford Ruether[16] are an important exchange in explaining Merton's own views on the relationship between activism and faith, not because (as they are sometimes read) they indicate that he was having doubts about his own calling but because they show Merton's profound frustration at being so deeply misunderstood by someone who shared so many of his own political and theological sympathies. In that exchange Ruether challenged Merton's monastic commitment suggesting that his "agrarian romanticism" did not take seriously enough the principalities and powers of the world, and invited him to struggle against the "dehumanizing forces in the city of man." She even suggested he leave Gethsemani to enter into the political fray full time.

Merton accused her of confusing her intellectual world with the real world, of preferring shadows to realities. "I wonder if you realize," he told her, "that you (at least from your letters) are a very academic, cerebral, abstract type. You talk about God's good creation, the goodness of the body, and all that, but I wonder if you have any realization at all of the fact that by working on the land a person is deeply and sensually involved with matter. . . . It is not romanticism at all, my friend. It is something you city people need, and need very badly indeed. . . . In actual fact, is there anything you can do in the city more effectively than I can do in the country, to stop the war in Vietnam? . . . My negative ideas about political life today are trying precisely to say that political action is too often rendered futile by the massive corruption and dishonesty and fakery which neutralize it everywhere. But I do not mean by that to say that political action is ineffective and hopeless: just that something else is needed."[17]

For Merton it was not a matter of rejecting historical responsibility or of equating the activity of the principalities and powers with history itself. The problem, he tells Reuther, "is not just one of false spirituality verses incarnation, but much more dangerously, of a false and demonic parody of creation and incarnation and redemption, a demonic parody of the Kingdom: and this is where a naive optimism about technology is a source of great problems. True historical responsibility cannot coexist with a blindness on this crucial point."[18]

I quote these passages at length because Merton is making a distinction here that is central to his witness: it is not enough simply to stand up to the principalities and powers of the world, one must dismantle within oneself those forces that set up a demonic parody of the Kingdom. We must resist the temptation to equate the confidence we acquire by swimming with the historical tide with actual prophetic insight. It's not enough to see through others' pretensions, we must see through our own, and that means we cannot simply enter the political arena with the hope of defeating falsehood if we are carrying the germ of falsehood within ourselves.

Merton's letter continues: "Certainly the demons down here are small-time. But it is by confronting them that a monk has to open the way to his own kind of involvement in the big-time struggle, or, as Vahanian said the other day, to be effectively iconoclastic in the modern world. I am personally keenly aware that if I threw up the sponge down here and went out to engage in something ostensibly more effective, it would be a real betrayal not of abstract obligations but of the Kingdom, in which the monastic life, however marginal, retains its importance."[19]

I am reminded here of Yuri Zhivago's remarks when he is brought in for questioning by the activist Strelnikov. The dedicated Bolshevik suggests that Yuri is either a traitor or a deserter because he has neither joined the revolution nor fought against it. Yuri replies (I am paraphrasing here), "Don't you think I haven't been grappling with these issues all my life? And wouldn't it be odd if I had not by now reached some conclusion? Only I can't put them into a couple of words. So permit me to leave without having it out with you. I have no excuses to make."[20] Merton had no excuses to make.

Years later Ruether described this exchange as an instance of two people talking past one another. "I see Thomas Merton and myself like two ships that happened to pass each other on our respective journeys. For a brief moment we turned our search lights on each other with blazing intensity. Then, when we sensed that we were indeed going in different directions, we began to pass each other by. Our future correspondence might have been cordial and even fruitful, but not of the same existential urgency. So for those who see this as the beginning of what might have been a beautiful relationship, my guess is, probably not."[21]

Professor Ruether graciously sent me the then-unpublished essay and remarked in her letter, "My relation with Thomas

Merton was at a very early stage in my own development as a scholar in theology, when I was looking for honest feed-back from Catholic thinkers of repute of a kind that was not easy to find at the time. For that reason I had what in retrospect sounds like a confrontational tone to the letters. It was in my understanding an entirely intellectual conversation, and thus the suggestion in some books on Merton of a personal relationship of great challenge to him may be an appropriate insight for Merton in retrospect, but does not correspond at all to my own side of the experience."[22]

Ruether, I think it is fair to say, was on her way toward a career as a distinguished breakthrough feminist theologian, while Merton was on his way to his hermitage and into further solitude. Ruether was finding her calling as a scholar; Merton was making yet another inward turn.

CHAPTER TWELVE

ZEN AS NEGATIVE DIALECTICS

Martin Heidegger once noted that the problem of modernity was not that we had forgotten the question of Being, but that we had forgotten that we had forgotten the question of Being. And although Merton respected Heidegger, studied his works, and admired his analysis of man's "desire to fall into the world in order to evade an inner dread of death,"[1] he ultimately found his philosophy "confused," and once even joked to a friend that Heidegger knew "nothing about Being."

Merton could say this because, from a contemplative perspective, there is nothing to know about Being. It can't be understood. It's a metaphor, not a concept. To explain its phenomenological structure in weighty tomes is to engage in a form of scholasticism that reveals exactly how little about Being one actually understands. Poetry is a far better medium for ontological investigations. Zen Koans even better.

The difference in perspectives between Merton and Heidegger is wonderfully illustrated in the different way the two men read the pre-Socratics. Heidegger saw Herakleitos as the first exponent of fundamental ontology; whereas, Merton saw him as a holy rebel. "He was," Merton wrote, "a contemporary of Aeschylus and of the victorious fighters of Marathon, but unlike the poets who wrote and sang in the dawn of the Attic Golden age, Herakleitos was a tight-lipped and cynical pessimist who viewed with sardonic contempt the political fervor of his contemporaries"[2]

Herakleitos, Merton reminds us, spoke for the mysterious, the unutterable, and the excellent, for the logos which was the true law of all being—not a static rigid form, but a dynamic principle of harmony-in-conflict. And he did this to awaken the mind of his disciples to a reality that was right before their eyes but that for some reason they were incapable of seeing.[3]

Herakleitos anticipated the principle problem of modernity. He saw that most people were deluded by polymathy—the learning of many things, the constant succession of novel truths, opinions, fresh doctrines, and revolutions. This multiplicity confused them with its vain appearance of sophistication and expertise. In reality, this whirl of activity is a form of intellectual and spiritual "sleep" that "deadens all capacity for the flash of mighty intuition by which the multiplicity is suddenly comprehended as one. The wise man must cling to the logos and to his unity with those who are aware of the logos, so he can bear witness to the 'common' thought and thereby win the 'greater portion.'"[4]

For Merton, faith does not lead to the recovery of any ontology but to the transformation of life and of human relations in the light of a God who is outside any predication, who is not a being but wholly other. Being is not structured but continually reforming itself as the manifestation of an unknown and unknowable mystery. It is not a philosophical category but a metaphor for the all-encompassing. One spoke best about it when one didn't speak about it at all. Silence was its language, ritual its vernacular, and the monastery its home. If it revealed itself in and through our living; nevertheless, it cannot be reduced to mere reverence for life.[5]

Merton explained the practical implications of this position more fully at a retreat for nuns in 1968 when he declared: "We don't have to follow anybody's line. We don't have to choose either nineteenth-century conservatism or one of the two brands of progressive ideas, liberal or Marxist. They are not expressly political, but there's a sort of political orientation behind them. People who take on a Marxist type approach, like some of the French Catholics, no matter how sharp their social criticism is, really end up in a political structure. For these people, the prophetic life and the radical Christian life and the eschatological life lead only to revolution. But it's not a free choice. What they are doing is accepting a choice dictated by Marxist ideology. It's not like the Russian situation at all, it's very French. So I think we have to be very careful of the people who simply equate the prophetic choice with the Marxist choice. That's very easy for a certain kind of Christian to do."[6]

So how does one attain to the true prophetic line?

"We just let Christ be faithful to us," Merton explains. "If we live with that kind of mind, we are prophetic. We become prophetic when we live in such a way that our life is an experience of the infallible fidelity of God. That's the kind of prophecy we are called to, not the business of being able to smell the latest fashion ten years before it happens. It is simply being in tune with God's mercy and will. . . . In other words, if we trust God to act in us, God will act in us. This is how our lives become prophetic. Prophecy is not a technique, it is not about telling someone else what to do. If we are completely open to the Holy Spirit, then the Spirit will be able to lead us where God wants us to go. Going along that line, our lives will become prophetic."[7]

Merton's answer here implies that although there may not be any single right answer in the abstract to such questions, there are single right answers for particular individuals in specific contexts. Each of us is called to certain tasks and responsibilities—indeed, to particular vocations that nobody can define for us from outside the realm of our own sphere of knowledge and experience. In fact, Merton goes so far as to say that doing God's will is not even necessarily doing "the right thing." God does not demand from us perfection in the abstract but obedience in the concrete. Transformative political action emerges from an instinctual defense of human truth against vested interests rationalized as ideals. It emerges from the brave man's unmasking of pretense and folly.

Both Buddhist and Christian monks share a suspicion of the interpretative powers of the mind. Both see ideology as a manifestation of the human predilection to illusion built upon false consciousness. In order to think clearly or even perceive honestly, a kind of spiritual turning or metanoia has to take place that exposes the limitations of the mind. Otherwise, one remains hypnotized by whatever interpretive system feeds one's sense of identity and, one's intellectual pride is magnified. Ascetic disciplines assault this hubris directly through a studied resistance to any and all forms of psychological tyranny.[8]

And so Merton turned to Zen as a way of thwarting dualistic thinking. Zen did not engage in Hegelian turns of logic but rather pointed directly at the unthought alternative. Zen mind was beginner's mind, not tactician's mind or dialectician's mind. One overcame false antinomies by instantly apprehending a larger pattern within which conflicting views simply dissolved as oppositions. Zen could not be employed as a means for furthering anyone's personal self-interest. In Zen there were no villains, nor easy answers. Only impossible questions and infinite self-responsibility—just like Cistercian monasticism!

In a powerful little parable titled "The Fasting of the Heart," based upon a translation from Chuang Tzu, Merton made clear the differences between his contemplative approach to social change and those of his politicized contemporaries. As the story goes, Yen Hui, a favorite disciple of Confucius, decided to leave his master to enter politics and save a state that was being destroyed by a corrupt king. Confucius asks him how he intends to bring about justice, given the hard heart of the king. Yen Hui replied: "Instead of directly opposing him, I will maintain my own standards interiorly, but outwardly I will appear to yield. I will appeal to the authority of tradition and to the examples of the past, He who is interiorly uncompromising is a son of heaven just as much as any ruler. I will not rely on any teaching of my own, and will consequently have no concern about whether I am approved or not. I will eventually be recognized as perfectly disinterested and sincere. They will all come to appreciate my candor, and thus I will be an instrument of heaven in their midst."[9]

This is an eloquent synopsis of Gandhian Satyagraha, or "Truth Force," the strategy Martin Luther King and the Southern Christian Leadership Conference employed in the early days of the civil rights movement. It is a recipe for humility that tempers one's ambitions while heightening one's sense of responsibility. Only if one stops thinking tactically can one begin to question one's own ends. One steps back and begins to see things from a perspective outside of time. One acquires, in other words, a critical point of view that acknowledges a *telos* greater than one's ambitions. And so one can suffer out the consequences of short-term failures confident in the knowledge that worldly struggle is itself a purgation, and hence the way to liberation from false values.

But in Merton's parable, Confucius ultimately rejects this approach as too limited, telling Yen Hui that it might succeed in superficially persuading the king to conform to his words, but there would be no real change in his heart. When the young disciple asks what then ought he do, Confucius suggests fasting—but not the usual fast observed by the conventionally religious. He suggests a fast of the heart.

Chuang Tzu explains: "The goal of fasting is inner unity. This means hearing, but not with the ear; hearing, but not with the understanding; hearing with the spirit, with your whole being. The hearing that is only in the ears is one thing. The hearing of the understanding is another. But the hearing of the spirit is not limited to any one faculty, to the ear, or to the mind. Hence it demands the emptiness of all the faculties. And when the faculties are empty, then the whole being listens. There is then a direct grasp of what is right there before you that can never be heard with the ear or understood with the mind. Fasting of the heart empties the faculties, frees you from limitation and from preoccupation. Fasting of the heart begets unity and freedom."

Yen Hui replies, "I see. What was standing in my way was my own self-awareness. If I can begin this fasting of the heart, self-awareness will vanish. Then I will be free from limitation and preoccupation! Is that what you are telling me?"

"Yes," says Confucius. "That's it! . . . If you follow human methods, you can get away with deception. In the way of Tao, no deception is possible. . . . You are familiar with the wisdom of those who know, but you have not yet learned the wisdom of those who know not. Look at this window: it is nothing but a hole in the wall, but because of it the whole room is full of light. So when the faculties are empty, the heart is full of light. Being full of light it becomes an influence by which others are secretly transformed."[10]

Here in a nutshell is Merton's contemplative response to the civil rights and peace movements of the sixties. It is not enough to employ nonviolence as a tool for justice if it leads you to believe that you are morally superior to your enemies. Motive is as important as results.

In the late sixties the progressive social movements were at a turning point. As their nonviolent strategies began to fail, they were being tempted to turn away from their search for purity of intention and embrace power politics. But if they followed this path, Merton warned, their true revolutionary potential would disappear and they would become merely a collection of various interest groups.

In his essay "Events and Pseudo-Events" (1967) Merton remarked: "Our choice is not that of being pure and whole at the mere cost of formulating a just and honest opinion. Mere commitment to a decent program of action does not lift the curse. Our real choice is between being like Job, who *knew* he was stricken, and Job's friends who did not know they were stricken too—though less obviously than he. (So they had answers!) To justify ourselves is to justify our sin and to call God a liar."[11]

The vocation of the dissident, like that of the monk, is the vocation of Job. The dissident must resist the lies of his or her comforters that stand between him and the truth—that sing in his ears and do his thinking for him. "One goes into the desert," Merton tells us, "to vomit up the interior phantom, the doubter, the double. . . . The ascesis of solitude is, then, a deep therapy which has uncovered the ascetic archetype in man."[12] Monastic formation, like Zen training, is a turning away from all that is not soul force—giving up all one's projects and self-justifications to stand like Job before God in naked need and incomprehension. It is a way of defeating "political" logic altogether by confronting it with a more inclusive sensibility.

Insofar as Merton attempted to live out the full implications of this view of politics as illusion, his life at Gethsemani became, like Thoreau's at Walden Pond, an experiment in living. "The real hope," he wrote, "is not in something we think we can do, but in God who is making something good out of it in some way we cannot see. If we can do his will, we will be helping this process. But we will not necessarily know all about it beforehand."[13] And so as the old cultural order began to crumble, Merton assured those who were struggling against the commercialization and politicization of all things sacred that the good they sacrificed for was not a fragile historical project that might or might not succeed, but an unshakable transhistoric reality that could never be defeated.

CHAPTER THIRTEEN

JOURNEY TO THE EAST

Merton left Gethsemani in the fall of 1968 for a several-month tour of Asia—ostensibly to give an address to an international monastic conference in Bangkok, Thailand, in December. But he extended the trip to include visits to various Buddhist and Cistercian monasteries throughout Asia and even addressed a Spiritual Summit Conference in Calcutta a few weeks before traveling to Bangkok.

This was Merton's first—and, as fate would have it, last—extended trip since entering the monastery in 1941. It was also a journey to the west as Merton made stops in California, New Mexico, and Alaska in hopes of locating a spot for a more solitary hermitage. Due to his fame, Gethsemani was getting to be a very busy place with many visitors and much correspondence. It was Merton's intention to keep Gethsemani as his address but live part of the year in the western hermitage, which would then also be available as a retreat house.

As his journals from this time indicate, Merton's reading on this trip was an eclectic blend of Asian spiritual classics—the *Brahma Sutra*, the poetry of Milarepa—and some modern works—the novellas of Nathaniel West and Anais Nin, an essay on Michel Foucault, *Negations* by Herbert Marcuse, and *The Opening of the Wisdom-Eye* by the Dalai Lama among others.

Merton's journal entries from the trip were also wide ranging and speculative. He juxtaposed passages from Nathaniel West with accounts of his meetings with the Dalai Lama. In an informal talk in Calcutta in October Merton offered this recipe for interfaith dialogue: "The deepest level of communication is not communication, but communion. It is wordless. It is beyond words, and it is beyond speech, and it is beyond concept. Not that we discover a new unity. We discover an older unity. My dear brothers, we are already one. But we imagine that we are not. And what we have to recover is our original unity. What we have to be is what we are."[1]

The high point of his trip, however, was his visit to the Polonnaruwa and the giant carved statues of the Buddha. "Looking at these figures," Merton wrote, "I was suddenly, almost forcibly jerked clean out of the habitual, half-tied vision of things, and an inner clearness, clarity, as if exploding from the rocks themselves, became evident and obvious. The queer evidence of the reclining figure, the smile, the sad smile of Ananda standing with arms folded (much more 'imperative' than Da Vinci's Mona Lisa because completely simple and straightforward). The thing about all this is that there is no puzzle, no problem, and really no 'mystery' . . . everything is emptiness and everything is compassion. I don't know when in my life I have ever had such a sense of beauty and spiritual validity running together in one aesthetic illumination."[2]

Some scholars have cited this passage as evidence that Merton in this last year of his life was on his way to becoming a Buddhist, but the entire thrust of the journal is a call for Buddhist and Christian and Muslim contemplatives to transcend their isolated traditions and to find God in accepting one another fully, completely, and without reservation.

Merton died a few days after writing these lines while attending an International Monastic Conference in Bangkok, Thailand, on December 10, 1968. He was killed by accidental electrocution in his room at the conference site. He had just given an address on "Marxism and Monastic Perspectives," which called once again for a vision that went beyond neo-Marxist hermeneutics and the need for a third position beyond both left and right—a "no-position" that suspended both. Merton died in midstride. Still working out the relationship between Buddhism, international politics, Christianity, Hinduism, Islam, monasticism, Zen, Marcuse, and Paul's Epistles—still seeking to articulate the misunderstood contemplative option.

His body was flown back to Kentucky in a United States Air Force jet along with the bodies of servicemen killed in the Vietnam War. He was buried, like the rest of the monks, under a simple white cross on the monastery grounds.

The tragedy of Merton's life was that he died too soon, both as a man and as a cultural alternative, to bring to full fruition the harvest of his labors. His work can be seen as a multivolume preface toward the renewal of Western spirituality through a rejection of the false values born of modernity and technological progress. When Merton died in 1968, he was not on the verge of any particular new turn in his thought so much as yet another deepening of it, a further maturing, a powerful, inclusive last phase.

The way he died gave birth to rumors that he had been assassinated, and it is easy to see the reasons for such suspicions. His death occurred the same year as the assassinations of Martin Luther King, Jr., and Robert Kennedy. In fact, King had been scheduled to make a retreat with Merton at Gethsemani earlier that year, and Robert Kennedy was making arrangements for Merton to give a series of talks at the White House.

And there were other connections. Like King and Kennedy, Merton was beginning to articulate a vision of social change and responsibility that went beyond both Christian fatalism and romantic rebellion to recoup traditional religious values on the far side of both neo-Marxism and traditional Enlightenment Liberalism. Like King and Kennedy, he was developing a response to contemporary alienation that factored in the longing for God and community.

In retrospect, 1968 looks more and more like the last gasp of what Robert Bellah once called "The Civil Religion of America" (Deadalus 1966). The assassinations seemed to signal an end to that whole set of evolving commitments to equality, human rights, and a life lived in accord with conscience. You need only to list the names of those who died in those ten short years prior to 1968 to get a virtual Who's Who of twentieth-century radical democratic individualism: Ernest Hemingway, William Faulkner, Richard Wright, John Steinbeck, William Carlos Williams, Robert Frost, Carl Sandburg, Langston Hughes, Robinson Jeffers, Zora Neale Hurston, Rachel Carson, e. e. cummings, Aldous Huxley, Flannery O'Connor, Dwight D. Eisenhower, Eleanor Roosevelt, John F. Kennedy, Malcolm X, Lyndon Johnson, Robert Kennedy, Martin Luther King, and, of course, Thomas Merton.

What these diverse figures held in common was a deep, all-consuming desire to renew the nation by holding it to the highest values of its creed. All of them believed that beneath society's customs and institutions, indeed beneath history itself, there was a law that human beings did not make, a cosmic order that transcended the will to power. They may have called this law by different names, but whatever their particular terms, each held to the notion that democratic societies were designed to thwart anyone or anything that would press its advantage over and against this larger, religious premise. None of these figures were moral or epistemological relativists. All of them possessed what Paul Tillich called "a theology of ultimate concern."

But if Merton, like so many other Americans of his time, was a defender of the democratic ideal, he was also an ascetic who saw religious faith and contemplation as a check against the natural hubris we all possess simply by virtue of being alive. His contribution to the American Civil Religion was a monk's warning against the forgetfulness of Being. He reminded us to be on guard against any insensitivity toward the eternal and against our own impatience with the unpresupposing surfaces of things.

The American modernist imagination, in its attempt to thwart the dehumanizing effects of mass culture, expressed a profound civic conscience. But Merton understood that it needed to evolve into a more self-consciously spiritual quest if it was ever going to survive. Indeed it needed to become an explicit search for purity of heart. By pointing out the unseen continuities between the American dream of a life lived in accord with conscience with the Desert Father's quest for right intention and the Zen master's search for a life lived in harmony with the Tao, Merton was beginning to articulate what amounted to an existential analytic of the sacred.

His death in 1968 came at the worst possible time. The sixties, which the novelist Robert Stone once described as a party that flowed out into the street, was coming to an abrupt and apocalyptic end. The official order tried to reestablish itself in a kind of confused and violent overreaction. Assassins gunned down the country's most transformative politicians, and scores of leaderless protestors were beaten senseless in the streets of Chicago.

In the years preceding 1968, virtually every institution in American society lost confidence in itself. Everything that was pushed just seemed to fall over: universities, corporations, even middle-class family life. But no unifying vision had accompanied the rebellion. Everyone was improvising. The culture had become a hodge-podge of uncoordinated responses to the void left by those in the official culture who had abdicated their authority. Merton's death was yet another nail in the coffin of the "American Civil Religion."

Watergate made things worse. Not only did it discredit the aura of the presidency, but it gave new authority to "tapes," "transcripts," and electronic devices. Mr. Butterfield's revelation that everything Nixon said had been "recorded on tape" was the oracle that announced the end of history as we knew it. In that moment, one could say, the era of electonic realities and "virtual" presidents began.

Thomas Merton never believed that technology could protect us from the frauds of history. He willingly submitted himself to the teachings of the Desert Fathers because the authority he sought was not the authority of position or of expertise, nor the authority of personal influence. He sought, rather, an inclusive and historically valid point of view, willingly subordinating himself to the past in order to find his place in the present.

Since his death, interest in Merton's alternative perspective has grown. The issues he raised have not been ignored.

Twenty-eight volumes of his essays, letters, journals, and talks have been published posthumously, and there are more on the way. His reading notebooks alone are expected to run to six volumes, and at last count there were already five full-length biographies.

But the turning point in Merton scholarship came in 1985 with the publication of the first volume of his collected letters, *The Hidden Ground of Love: Letters on Religious Experience and Social Concerns*, edited by William H. Shannon and published by Farrar, Straus, and Giroux. Although a small number of scholars and biographers previously had access to these materials, the publication of this collection revealed a side of Thomas Merton hitherto known only to a small cadre of initiates. Here was an intellectually engaged dynamo involved in a variety of contemporary issues, corresponding with thinkers from all backgrounds and traditions: from Freudian revisionists such as Erich Fromm, to Catholic activists Dorothy Day and Daniel Berrigan, to poets from South America such as Ernesto Cardenal, and even avant-garde novelists like Henry Miller. Subsequent volumes of his letters revealed an even larger pool of correspondents that included the Zen Buddhist D. T. Suzuki, the environmentalist Rachel Carson, the Russian dissident Boris Pasternak, and the Polish poet/émigré Czeslaw Milosz.

The significance of these letters does not derive from their diversity but from the deep unity that pervades them. In the midst of a radically plural, even fragmented age, Thomas Merton had begun the difficult task of uniting within himself all the various strands of a truly universal Catholicism. And he did this—not by theorizing a metatheology a la Teilhard de Chardin or a monomyth a la Joseph Campbell, but through an existential appropriation of the experiential wisdom of many different people. He wasn't seeking a system so much as a radical excavation of his own subjective life in order to overcome the false distinctions and inverted priorities of the secular world.

"If I can *unite in myself* the thought and devotion of Eastern and Western Christendom, the Greek and the Latin Fathers, the Russians and the Spanish mystics," he wrote, "I can prepare *in myself* the reunion of divided Christians. From that secret and unspoken unity in myself can eventually come a visible and manifest unity of all Christians. If we want to bring together what is divided, we cannot do so by imposing one division upon the other or absorbing one division into the other. But if we do this, the union is not Christian. It is political, and doomed to further conflict. We must contain all divided worlds in ourselves and transcend them in Christ."[3]

This ambition placed him closer in spirit to the religious experimentalism of Jack Kerouac, Allen Ginsberg, and Gary Snyder than it did the mainstream theologians of his day. But Merton never abandoned Christian orthodoxy; he just kept extending its parameters as his own sense of unity and identity increased. "The more I am able to affirm others, to say 'yes' to them in myself, by discovering them in myself and myself in them, the more real I am. I am fully real if my own heart says yes to everyone. I will be a better Catholic, not if I can refute every shade of Protestantism, but if I can affirm the truth in it and still go further. So too, with the Muslims, the Hindus, the Buddhists, etc. This does not mean syncretism, indifferentism, the vapid and careless friendliness that accepts everything by thinking of nothing. There is much that one cannot 'affirm' and 'accept,' but first one must say 'yes' where one really can."[4]

Merton did not merely seek philosophical coherence born of precise intellectual distinctions. He sought a personal appropriation of many points of view for the sake of a unified personal vision. When that vision surfaced in the public debates of his time, he often found himself in conflict with narrow, more partisan points of view. But when he exposed the obsolescence of the old categories, the new possibilities seemed more real than the obstacles standing in the way of their realization.

Thomas Merton's greatest contribution may have been to place himself at the intersection between twentieth-century skepticism and twelfth-century religious piety—living out the paradoxes as bravely as he could, refusing to give in to any view that would simply collapse one within the another. His life was a journey into the Self. Not the petty, personal self disoriented by "the modern," but the transcendental Self of Whitman, Lao Tzu, and the Desert Fathers—the Self that is eternally modern, that contains multitudes and embraces complexity. He could accept diversity because he had experienced first hand the unity that precedes all divisions.

CHAPTER FOURTEEN

POSTMODERN MERTON?

I t is hard to gauge how Thomas Merton might respond to specific contemporary issues if he were alive today. As we have seen, he was no ideologue, but took each issue apart, exposed the fallacies of the contending sides, and then attempted to let the truth stand on its own. He wasn't a system builder but a dissident; and he employed a rhetoric of discovery checked by a contemplative appeal to conscience to oppose positivist assertions. To extrapolate from his essays on the Cold War, say, his position on the so-called Culture Wars would be a bit of a presumption. We just don't know how he would have read the situation or the presumptions he might have chosen to expose.

We do know, however, that he sought to expose the myths of modernity, the misapplications of the principles of nonviolence, and the presumptions of "Kitsch" Catholicism. And so it is tempting to draw analogies between Merton's call for a postontological monasticism and the radical critique of classical metaphysics offered by postmodern and poststructuralist theorists. But it is *not* an apt comparison.

Merton's most likely response to Jacques Lacan's quip, "I think where I am not, therefore I am where I do not think"[1] would have been to let out a hardy Zen laugh in total agreement. The remark points to a serious flaw in the Cartesian world view; namely, that as human beings we do not experience ourselves as grounded by our thoughts, but rather suspended, as Pascal might say, between infinities. Lacan's aphorism mimics the religious insight that our subjectivity is never completely accessible to language, and so confirms our intuition that a part of us remains forever outside of our thoughts. Our egos are therefore doomed to a perpetual search for essence that can never be fulfilled.

In *New Seeds of Contemplation*, Merton says almost exactly the same thing, using different terms: "To say I was born in sin is to say I came into the world with a false self. I was born in a mask. I came into existence under a sign of contradiction, being someone that I was never intended to be and therefore a denial of what I am supposed to be. And thus I came into existence and nonexistence at the same time because from the very start I was something that I was not."[2]

But where Merton differs from Lacan is that he does not believe that our inability to unify thought and existence necessarily implies that we are always already alienated. In *Zen and the Birds of Appetite*, Merton insists that "another metaphysical consciousness is still available to us. It starts not from the thinking and the self-aware subject but from Being, ontologically beyond and prior to the subject-object division. Underlying the subjective experience of the individual, there is an awareness of Being. This awareness of Being is totally different from an awareness of self-consciousness. It has in it none of the split and alienation that occurs when the subject becomes aware of itself as a quasi-object."[3]

And so although Merton might agree that we are all born into illusory identities, indeed that our very notions of self are ipso facto fictions, he also believes we are all born into Being. Indeed, Being supersedes consciousness and contains it. There is no need to find ourselves, we merely have to overcome the illusion that we were ever lost. Or another way of putting this is that we must see through the claims of our illusory selves in order to identify with our infinitely more mysterious true selves—die to this world in order to be reborn into the actual one.

For Lacan, subjectivity *is* consciousness, and so the only self that exist *is* the illusory self—a quasi-object set off from all other objects. As a result, we can never find our "true" selves because the play of images that make up the sign systems that constitute culture are built upon the disassociation of ourselves from others. When we use language, we generate a myriad of significances that constitute the sound and fury of our lives. But there is no Being. No God. No silence. Only difference, tropes, and systems.

But for Merton the silent self (our real self) *is* accessible. There is a part of us that is not a striving but a listening. And that part can only be experienced if we recognize it as a part of the preexisting unity in all of creation. It is fine to speak about the subterfuges of the ego; psychoanalysis does a great job of this. But we experience our true selves, our silent selves, only in those moments when grace redeems existence from within our own despair. This is not a theoretical or even conscious achievement, but rather a flash of recognition, followed by a humbling sense that as bad as things may seem to us, all things are in their rightful place.

One of the purposes of religion is to make these moments more likely to occur by creating a psychological environment hospitable to contemplation. God must be free *not* to respond to man—just as man must be free not to respond to God—if true communion is to take place. If either side is forced into participating, there is, in essence, only one person there, therefore no revelation, no joy, and no love.

Poststructuralists, like Lacan, seldom emphasize the prerogative of the Other *not* to respond, and instead focus upon the impossibility of any language to compel assent. Although they seem to celebrate the arbitrary nature of the sign, poststructuralists are scandalized by it. Their Cartesian preoccupation with certainty and their conception of the self *as consciousness* simply precludes Merton's dialogic conception of the self as existing only in and through relationships. Even though consciousness per se can be explained better by a naturalist philosophy of mind than by psychoanalytic theory, antifoundationalists like Lacan remain focused upon the limitations of representative discourse.[4] Yet, by constantly seeking to expose what they perceive as creeping "metaphysics," they preempt religious revelation by insisting upon an antimetaphysic as "mystic" in its "foundationless" presumptions as any faith that ever existed.

The difference between the grammatologists and traditional mystics is that the "new" antimetaphysical metaphysicians believe themselves free from presumption and therefore suffer from a incorrectable theoretical vertigo. There is no palm at the end of their minds, as Wallace Stevens might have put it. And so all the great sources of plebeian religious solace and reform—conscience, intuition, social solidarity, and aesthetic feeling—have all been rendered arbitrary—politicized—naturalized—by postmodern thought. And yet Merton, as a mystic, understood that the logocentricism of the Gospels was always and already "under erasure." In fact, the logocentricism of the Gospels was not logocentricism at all, but precisely the radical recognition of a reality beyond all predication—the word made flesh.

In this sense Merton's ideas are totally antithetical to recent theoretical trends in the humanities and social sciences. His work is contextual, specific, unflinchingly existential. His continuing relevance to our time as a thinker, an activist, indeed as a metaphysician and moralist, grows out of the fact that he does not abandon reasoned ethical inquiry in order to expose false thinking. Schooled in the *nada* of St. John of the Cross, he begins from a position of absolute skepticism toward the Cartesian *cogito* and so finds the displacement of the bourgeois subject from the center of the self hardly revolutionary.

In fact, from Merton's Trappist point of view, any essentialist definition of the self misreads the human condition. Not because essences are in themselves folly, but because in essence we are all one. It is this primary ontological presumption that protects him from philosophical relativism and yet opens him to dialogue with others, whether they think in essentialist terms or nct.

Merton's ability to be an essentialist and existentialist at the same time can be understood best by looking at his ideas about language which derive largely from the linguistic theories of Brice Parain, a Catholic convert who was a close friend of Albert Camus and an important influence on the avant-garde filmmaker Jean-Luc Godard.[5]

Parain raised questions similar to those posed by the poststructuralists: Can language make sense if there is no God? What is the point of talking about truth or falsity if there is no referent—no metaphysical ground—no signified attached to the signifier? Merton rephrased these issues: "Is not man, in that case, reduced to putting together a series of more or less arbitrary noises in the solitude of a mute world? Are these noises anything more than the signals of animals and birds? True, our noises exist in a very complex on-going context of development and are richly associated with one another and with other cultural phenomena: but can they be true? Or are they merely incidents in a developing adventure that will one day end in some kind of meaning but which, for the time being, has none?"[6]

Parain's work began with such post-Hegelian quandaries, but it culminated in an existential-analytic similar to Merton's view that language must be used "to awaken in man the lucid anguish in which alone he is truly conscious of his condition and therefore able to revolt against the absurd. Then he will affirm, over against its 'unreasonable silence,' the human love and solidarity and devotion to life which give meaning to his own existence."[7] Put simply, in a fallen world, language responsibly employed can awaken us to an awareness of our own condition, to a lucid anguish that leads us to assert our humanity over and against the forces that oppose it.

In poststructuralist thought, this rebellion is accompanied by certain epistemological doubts that dissipate faith in one's self *as a self* and subtly undermine moral resolve. To speak or to write "grammatologically"[8]—to put ideas under erasure—is not an act of conscience per se but an evasion of the suffering that accompanies taking a stand or positing a value. The endlessly bracketed tropes offered by grammatologists are, quite simply, a form of decadence, a kind of intellectual formalism gone mad, a sort of reverse Zen: the Koan without the Enlightenment, the pointing finger but no moon.

Merton cites an entry in one of Camus's notebooks: "Peace would be living in silence. But there is conscience and the person; you have to speak. To love becomes hell."[9] To love truth, in the way Merton understands truth, becomes a kind of hell because it requires you to speak in a fallen language. The only way to avoid complicity with the ways of the world is to live in perfect interior silence or to adopt a perspective that renders all discourse philosophically mute. But, of course, neither of these "answers" is available to the Christian Apostle.

The crucifixion is love and suffering, communication and incomprehension, Hell and Heaven, History and Transcendence, all in one. It is an enactment, emblem, and symbol of the "lucid anguish" inherent in the human condition. To put it (or any other symbol for that matter) "under erasure" is to create a simulacra of "silence." But history demands of us something else altogether: witness, personhood, and sacrifice—however incomplete that sacrifice may ultimately turn out to be. The primary problem within Western philosophy is not that language itself inevitably leads to a false metaphysic but that lies, dissimulation, and pride thwart our relationships with one another, and mere philosophical *gnosis* is powerless to overcome this defect in our nature.

In his essay "Symbolism" Merton warns his readers not "to join in the triumphant, empty-headed crowing of advertising men and engineers of opinion"[10] who use words as an instrument of the will and thereby cannot express any other reality except a "knowledge of knowledge." Instead, he urges them to use language to bring humanity, nature, and God together in a living and sacred synthesis, to express and to encourage our acceptance of our own ontological roots in a mystery that transcends our individual egos. "When man is reduced to his empirical self as he is in a technological age," Merton wrote, "he cannot 'see' the symbols because he is incapable of interior response."[11]

This incapacity for interior response is really at the heart of much poststructuralist criticism. Its preoccupation with method attracts those who reject or never clearly understood the religious content at the heart of the Western Intellectual tradition. But rather than encouraging them to move more deeply into their own metaphysical longings to trace their existential discomforts back to their origins in the history of thought, deconstruction offers instant access to moral repudiation at bargain-basement prices.

This is the unfortunate and largely unforeseen consequence of the epistemological turn: the unity of gnosis and praxis, once at the heart of Western thought, has been replaced by an ersatz theoretical unity that does not actually exist. To return to the search for the sublime in action and in word, a kind of preliminary spiritual reeducation must take place. This is one of the reasons Merton's life and witness continue to be so important: they provide just such a primer.

Jean Baudrillard has argued in *Simulations* (1983) that the ultimate slogan of power in our "nonreferential" world is "Take your desires for reality." By this, he means that the last refuge of realism in our deconstructed age resides in attributing reality to our dreams. "I want it; therefore it exists." And this slender remnant of what was once Western metaphysical realism is all that keeps us from becoming nihilists or embracing asceticism. "Even the confusion of the reality principle with the desire principle is less dangerous 'than contagious hyperreality'" he tells us, "because one remains among principles, and there power is always right."[12]

In other words, as long as desire and reality are in dialogue with one another, the consumer society functions and naturalism makes sense. But once you perceive that no desire is in itself any more real than any other desire, you pass over into a skepticism that undermines the entire socioeconomic foundations of modern civilization.

To write with your desires, as many poststructuralists do, merely confirms the status quo. It is a concession to one's ordinary self, to impulse. It is not a true expression of the confusion that actually exists between who we think we are and who we might yet be, between the world that recreates us in its own practico-inert image and our own quasireligious longings for transcendence. And yet if we would only refuse to participate in the prevailing mythology of desire, like Merton and his fellow monks, we would realize that beneath the apparent order of nature lies a chaos of irrationality, confusion, pointlessness, and void—what Baudrillard calls "hyperreality." This chaos, Merton tells us, "is what immediately impresses itself upon the man who has denounced diversion."[13] And it is the first step in the spiritual life.

At its best, poststructuralist theory reveals the permanent irresolvability of certain intellectual dichotomies—such as presence and absence, teleology and genealogy—and challenges us to resist facile syntheses and onesided ideological critiques. On the other hand, Christian mysticism simply assumes the ultimate identity of those same philosophical antinomies and challenges us to experience their unity. When seen from the perspective of the paradox of the cross, from the eschatological point of view of a messianic "return," genealogy *is* teleology; absence *is* presence; the individual *is* universal. The Cross tropes any and all Hegelian totalizations or Derridian deconstructions. Like the sublime, it "yields up easier satisfactions for a more delayed and difficult reward." Its difficulty is an authentic mark of originality, "an originality that must seem eccentric until it usurps psychic space and establishes itself as a fresh center."[14] Christ crucified declares an openended universe at the very moment it overcomes the world; it is the ultimate expression of the human imagination: posturing, hurting, living, dying, enigmatic.

Postmodernists who begin by decentering human subjectivity from the center of human experience bar themselves from such metaphors necessary for a rich description of human life, and so fall back upon their only absolute—theory—to describe their search for ideological excesses. But in the process, they abandon concrete experience to the purview of literal language and so have nothing to say to particular individuals living in particular, contingent worlds requiring sacrifice, decision, and choice—nothing beyond the sweeping, utopian admonition to begin again from the bottom up. Spiritual religion as poesis, however, does have something to say. It encourages us to overcome distracting projects and illusory preoccupations in order to attend to a *telos* outside ourselves and to circumstances revealed in and through the needs of others. This is what Merton means by "purity of heart."

If we try to become literalists by deconstructing the ontotheological biases built into language itself or denuding our sign systems of all symbolic content, we do not overcome myth; we simply create new, more disguised forms of it that require yet more deconstructing. But if we can learn to respond to words like the mystics do, not merely as signs but as symbols, then we might be able to defeat our pride long enough to look into one another's eyes.

In his essay "From Pilgrimage to Crusade" Merton wrote, "Our task now is to learn that if we can voyage to the ends of the earth and find *ourselves* in the aborigine who most differs from ourselves, we will have made a fruitful pilgrimage. That is why pilgrimage is necessary, in some shape or other. Mere sitting at home and meditating on the divine presence is not enough. We have to come to the end of a long journey and see that the stranger we meet there is no other than ourselves—which is the same as saying we find Christ in him. For if the Lord is risen, as He said, He is actually or potentially alive in every man. Our pilgrimage to the Holy Sepulcher is our pilgrimage to the stranger who is Christ, our fellow pilgrim and brother."[15]

This sense of a shared spiritual identity common to all people because it is deeper than our differences explains why Merton does not adopt in his writing the voice of the philosopher, theologian, or even spiritual "specialist." He wants to speak from the source of his own being, which, if achieved, will resonate with the being of others. When you look closely at any one of Merton's books, there is a studied evasion of abstract categories because he knows that his readers still live within their own souls and need to experience the sublime on their own terms. In our time only the most heroic souls—Samuel Beckett, Franz Kafka, Anna Ahkmatova, Rainier Rilke, and Boris Pasternak—have had the courage to invent their own idioms of redemption and, thereby, rescue the symbol from the sign and the person from the individual. Their works, like Merton's books, are part of the secret history of the twentieth century—expressions of an emerging monastic, or should we call it "eschatological"—underground.

In his journal published under the title *Vow of Conversation* in 1965, Merton copied down the following quotation from Karl Jaspers: "Once I envision world history or life's entirety as a kind of finite totality, I can only act on the basis of sham knowledge, in distortion of actual possibilities, far from reality, vague about facts, achieving nothing but confusion and advancing in directions altogether different from those I wanted. . . . Whenever my knowledge is chained to total concepts, whenever my actions are based on a specific world view, I am distracted from what I am really able to do. I am cheated of the present for the sake of something imagined, past or future, rather than real."[16]

The monk, like the poet, dissents from such totalizing "logic" to become a living, breathing demythologist of the given. Contemplation, prayer, self-criticism, humility, the study of scripture, participation in tradition, the ingestion of one's grief, and the abandonment of ambition, enable one to perceive the actual. Poststructuralist theory mimics this dissent and so, ironically, makes it harder for us to transcend metaphysics; whereas, Merton as a Christian apostle remains absolutely, paradoxically, teleologically placed.

CHAPTER FIFTEEN

CONCLUSION

The meaning of my life is not to be looked for merely in the sum total of my own achievements. It is seen only in the complete integration of my achievements and failures with the achievements and failures of my own generation, and society, and time. It is seen, above all, in my integration in the mystery of Christ.

—Thomas Merton

When I began this study, Thomas Merton appeared to me to be the Lone Ranger of Desert Spirituality, challenging Americans to embrace a strenuous faith that did not fear poverty, chastity, or obedience, a faith that renewed—what Perry Miller once called the "Augustinian strain of American piety." With one honest book, *The Seven Storey Mountain*, Merton had boldly refuted both the soulless instrumentalism of the postwar technocrats and the insipid religious bromides offered by their positive-thinking preacher cohorts.

But the closer I looked into Merton's place in American intellectual history, the clearer it became that he was not particularly unique in either his ideas nor in his religious commitments. In fact, *The Seven Storey Mountain* was only one of many postwar books advocating a return to religion. The very same year Merton's book came out, no less a figure than Arnold Toynbee published an abridged edition of *A Study of History* that insisted Western civilization's only hope for survival consisted in a return to God. The English translation of Dietrich Bonhoeffer's *The Cost of Discipleship* appeared a year later, and Paul Tillich's *The Shaking of the Foundations* the year after that. Clare Boothe Luce even published the story of her conversion to Catholicism a year before Merton's.

To find anything original in Merton's writing, one has to look to his essays written in the late fifties and early sixties. But even there he was not particularly innovative as a theorist. The linking of religion to social activism in a "muscular" Christianity had already been advocated by Walter Rauschenbush, Dorothy Day, and any number of African American clergymen from Mordecai Johnson to Vernon Johns. As for his dialogue with Buddhism, Allan Watts and Gary Snyder had been on their journeys to the East for years. And Allen Ginsberg, Jack Kerouac, Henry Miller, and Norman O. Brown all embraced various forms of "mysticism" as antidotes to postindustrial ennui.

No, what made Merton remarkable and continues to recommend him as a writer and spiritual master to this day has less to do with his originality—he was after all an Orthodox Catholic virtually his entire adult life—than it does with his telling psychological interpretations and his sincere attempt to practice what he preached. Thomas Merton was no mere theorist of the sacred but a God-intoxicated man, a practicing contemplative, who spent his life within a physically demanding and spiritually rigorous religious order. His passionate embrace of silence, poverty, and chastity earned him the right to report back to the secular world what he had seen from the far side of worldly ambition. His poetry, journals, letters, and essays move unflinchingly further and further behind the facade of every popular illusion and facile self-justification.

In one of his last talks, Merton remarked: "In speaking for monks, I am really speaking for a very strange kind of person, a marginal person, because the monk in the modern world is no longer an established person with an established place in society. The marginal man accepts the basic irrelevance of the human condition, an irrelevance which is manifested above all by the fact of death. The marginal person, the monk, the displaced person, the prisoner, all these people live in the presence of death, which calls into question the meaning of life."[1] As a monk, in other words, Merton looked directly into the face of death in himself, trying to find something deeper than death, because, as he put it: "There is something deeper than death, and the office of the monk or the marginal person or the poet is to go beyond death even in this life, to go beyond the dichotomy of life and death and to be, therefore, a witness to life."[2] This is the calling of the Apostle.

But to go beyond the dichotomy of life and death you must step outside the phantasmagoria of history, and to do this you need to acquire some standard for the transvaluation of worldly values. Merton found that standard in what Jesus had called "the Kingdom of God." But he knew that it was not enough simply to postulate this realm as a "regulative concept." He had to live a life in accord with its principles. Faith in our time demanded a brave recognition of the absurdity of the human condition.

But unlike other dissidents, Merton believed that "transgressive" or "counterhegemonial" cultural practices did not offer a significant enough challenge to a world dominated by an amoral, instrumentalist mentality. The idol of material progress could only be called into question by exposing the entire set of economic, social, and psychological arrangements as pandering to self-interest. Merton came to the conclusion, at a very early age, that if he was ever going to live a life in service to man or to God, he would have to "give up everything." And what was original about him, was that he did just that.

As a result, his writings effortlessly exposed the flawed "anthropology" at the heart of the materialist world views dominating both the Eastern and Western Blocs. For him, the only alternative to power politics was the way of nonviolent, noncooperation with evil as practiced by Gandhi's soldiers of truth and Martin Luther King's Southern Leadership Conference. History would, of course, later confirm his strategy through the victories of Vaclav Havel's Civic Forum and Lech

Walesa's Solidarity Movement, and in the brave, democratic rebellion of the heroes of Tiennamen Square.

Although Merton died before these later movements came into prominence, he had argued for years that the only way to defeat totalitarian regimes was to embrace solitude as a living protest against the prerogatives of empire. He did not believe a mere changing of the economic guard would effect any final change; a spiritual revolution needed to take place. The Desert Fathers, although they didn't know it, actually did build a new world from within the shell of the old, preparing the way for the personalist humanism of the Renaissance by refusing to compromise with the false values of their age. From the point of view of their worldly Roman peers, they must have appeared totally irrelevant, but today we know that they were the bridge between classical civilization and the modern world.

Merton wanted to build a similar bridge between the twelfth and twentieth centuries, between Christian contemplation and contemporary existentialism, between the perennial wisdom of the East and the materialism of the West. As he put it in his Asian Journal: "Everything I think or do enters into the construction of a mandala. It is the balancing of experience over the void."[3] Merton did not advocate a return to a simpler world but an increasingly inclusive dialogue between seemingly contradictory worlds. Not because he was interested in inclusiveness as an end in itself, but because he thought that he could discover his true self only in and through dialogue with others.

Following through on the modernist project to "make it new," he tried to figure out the meaning the Trappist spirituality held for his own life and times—struggling to understand the Prodigal Son as a story about himself and the Resurrection as an intimate anagogical truth. To do this with intellectual honesty, he had to reread the Bible within the context of competing religious traditions and the expanding secular influence ushered in by socioeconomic modernization.

By refusing the heady wine of metatheory and embracing his own personal search for meaning in our postmodern, postliberal world, Merton became the representative of a new kind of global ecumenicalism that was working itself out—not in councils or in committees, but in the souls of individual seekers. And so although he was cloistered, he found himself at the very center of the search for the interior source of species awareness that had inspired and confounded thinkers as diverse as Karl Marx, Sigmund Freud, Carl Jung, Mircea Eliade, Martin Buber, and D. T. Suzuki.

Merton described his own sense of calling this way: "My own peculiar task in my Church and in my world has been that of the solitary explorer who, instead of jumping on all the latest bandwagons at once, is bound to search the existential depths of faith in its silences, its ambiguities, and in those certainties which lie deeper than the bottom of anxiety. In those depths there are no easy answers, no pat solutions to anything. It is a kind of submarine life in which faith sometimes mysteriously takes on the aspect of doubt when, in fact, one has to doubt and reject conventional and superstitious surrogates that have taken the place of faith. On this level, the division between Believer and Unbeliever ceases to be so crystal clear. It is not that some are all right and others are all wrong: all are bound to seek in honest perplexity. Everybody is an Unbeliever more or less! Only when this fact is fully experienced, accepted, and lived with, does one become fit to hear the simple message of the Gospel—or of any other religious teaching."[4]

As this passage makes clear, the most singular aspect of Merton's witness was his unflagging need to expose bad faith in fashions and in antifashions, in belief and in unbelief, indeed to chase down inauthenticity whenever and wherever it reared its ugly, complacent head and demand accountability. In the process of calling everyone's bluff—including his own— he discovered a hidden unity behind the bogus distinctions born of human pride.

The real story of our time, he insisted time and again, was not that we have moved beyond ideology or arrived at the end of history, but that we have succeeded in fooling ourselves into believing that we have already done both when our lives are actually more theoretical, abstract, and morally compromised than they have ever been before, ideological to the core, planned, processed, and managed by experts, and "historicized" beyond belief. Our egos have not dissipated into a postmodern semiotic sea of pure possibility, but have actually hardened into tiny, little rocks of self-interest—inflexible, indestructible. The postwar world did not give birth to a renaissance of inwardness, but to an explosion of popular distractions. As a consequence, the emerging worldwide middle class is desperately attempting to compensate, through the fulfillment of its own private ambitions, for the overwhelming unhappiness of its lost intellectual soul.

Francis Fukuyama, in his influential essay of 1989 "The End of History?" looked at these developments and concluded that liberal democracies offered the maximum in human freedom. "In the future," he wrote, "we risk becoming secure and self-absorbed last men, devoid of thymotic striving for higher goals in pursuit of private comforts. But the opposite danger exists as well, namely, that we will return to being first men engaged in bloody and pointless prestige battles, only this time with modern weapons."[5]

What Fukuyama calls liberal democracy, Merton saw as a runaway technopoly ruled by principalities of the air. Hardly liberal, even the most democratic of modern political regimes run on a very tiny ledger of received ideas. Modern leaders and liberal institutions are not tolerant of dissent, so much as skilled at doing away with it. History does not end with these managed democracies run by public relations firms, anymore than it ended with the Roman Empire or the Russian Revolution. From Merton's perspective, the struggle for human liberation has just begun.

Or rather, it never ends. The idea that history functions as some sort of precategory to all thought is itself a modern idea, and when pushed too far becomes an out and out capitulation to the powers that be. "We are living," Merton wrote, "under a tyranny of untruth which confirms itself in power and establishes a more and more total control over men in proportion as they convince themselves they are resisting error. Our submission to plausible and useful lies involves us in greater and more obvious contradictions, and to hide these from ourselves we need greater and ever less plausible lies. The basic falsehood is the lie that we are totally dedicated to the truth."[6]

Milan Kundera, the Czech novelist, made this same point in his Jerusalem address "The Novel and Europe," first published in the *New York Review of Books* in the spring of 1985. In that essay, Kundera argued that we are living in an age of epidemic self-deception. He diagnosed the great spiritual ill of our time as "the modernization of stupidity." In the old world, he explained, stupidity was simple ignorance, illiteracy: one didn't know anything, but one could learn. In the modern world, stupidity has evolved into a new more virulent form: the nonthought of received ideas. There is just as much ignorance today as ever, but individuals hide it behind phrases acquired through superficial contact with the mass media, opinion makers, and the schools.

This stupidity is harder to correct because the people who hold to it—largely the new middle class—consider themselves so well informed, so honest and sincere, that they stubbornly resist not only any attempt to forge more telling and inclusive syntheses but the difficult act of actual thought itself. This false confidence in their own powers of discernment constitutes the real "revolt of the masses," and it is the reason authentic social reforms are so much more difficult to come by these days than are revolutions in taste or popular crusades. The new middle class define themselves not in reference to any particular set of duties or responsibilities but in reference to particular images and associations, likes and dislikes, produced largely by the media.

If Kundera's diagnosis is correct, then the real enemy is not ignorance but folly. It isn't because we don't know things that our reforms fail; it is because we believe things that aren't true. And so we don't register the true complexities of matters at hand or acknowledge the subtle moral-spiritual dimensions inherent in our actions. The Nazi plague and the Red Menace were not failures of intelligence but rank capitulations to illusion.

Kundera found his antidote to folly in the wisdom of the novel, or, as he put, in "the deprecated legacy of Cervantes."[7] The novel's dialogical form could still pierce preconceptions, dramatize differences, and thereby preserve, if only for a saving remnant of serious readers, the possibility of personhood

in an age of anxiety. Merton found his antidote in the deprecated legacy of the Desert Fathers who—like Henry David
Thoreau—retired to the wilderness to see if they might not
discover on their own what was real and what was true. Their
lives were a protest against collective illusions and embodied
a very practical and unassuming wisdom that can if we let it
"reopen the sources that have been polluted or blocked altogether by the accumulated mental and spiritual refuse of our
technological barbarism."[8]

The problem, as Merton sees it, is not that Western civilization has been taken over by a repressive ideology nor is it, as
Nietzsche argued, that we have been infected with nihilism
created by the Christian devaluation of the world. From Merton's perspective, our problems stem from a general, psychological migration, since the late Renassiance, away from any
identification with our silent selves. The increasing focus of
individuals on human agency over human *being* has given
reign to a multitude of distracting, if well-intentioned, reform
movements. Although necessary in their time, the sheer per-
vasiveness of these movements, their radical success in doing
away with the old hierarchical mind set, has made it very difficult for us to grasp the meaning of symbols, to live in faith,
and to recognize the claims of conscience.

For Merton, the antidote to this confusion—and to the
worldwide psychological depression it has brought about—
was not collectivism or individual protest but a return to contemplative living. In the insights of the Desert Fathers, in
their radical retreat from the lies of a dying empire, in their
reflections, stories, rhetorical inversions, and dark wisdom,
Merton found the existential completion to the partial truths
offered by the masters of twentieth-century modernism. They
provided a model for his own resistance to a world so proud of
its demystification of classical metaphysics that it was incapable of getting any perspective on itself. They offered a way
of response to a world liberated from God but fallen into an
overwhelming sense of its own temporality.

Nietzsche's call to stop boldly at the surfaces of things may
once have been a liberating strategy, a way of not getting
sucked into the superficial mythologies of nation states, races,

or religions. But to employ such an approach in a postmodern context plays into the hands of the media masters, demagogues, and advertisers who exploit our impatience with the unprepossessing surface of the real in order to sell us more glamorous simulations—images, "news," and virtual realities, that do not point to any truth within ourselves but rather generate a thirst for further diversions and surface complexities.

We may all experience the "nada" of the mystic everyday, but we will never know it as *nada* if we don't possess the language capable of disclosing it to us. If we go about calling the contemporary spiritual wasteland a utopia, we will never know who we are. The media aggravates this condition by perscribing the false remedy of perpetual self-forgetting through entertainment. For Merton, interior silence is the way back to reality. "The greatest need of our time," he has written, "is to clean out the enormous mass of mental and emotional rubbish that clutters our minds and makes of all political and social life a mass illness. Without this housecleaning we cannot begin to see. Unless we see, we cannot think."[9]

Thomas Merton exposed the false metaphysic at the heart of our pandemic modern materialisms and by so doing increased our energy and morale by demonstrating that our "anxiety" and "bad faith" did not derive entirely from our own moral failings but were a product of the endless politicization and commercialization of every hitherto sacred cultural practice. And yet Merton did not prophesy the end of man nor the death of God. Like the Desert Fathers, he made do with what symbolism remained, joined the church, mastered its contemplative tradition, and spoke out and through its symbolism, confident that his witness as a poet and as a monk, as a dissident and as a marginal man, would resonate with others seeking the truth.

The way to find the real world, he insisted, is not to measure and observe what is outside us but to discover our own inner ground. That "ground," that "world," where we are mysteriously present at once to our selves and to others, is not a visible, objective, and determined structure with fixed laws and demands. It is, Merton tells us, "a living and self-creating mystery of which we ourselves are a part, to which we our-selves are our own unique doors."[10]

The via negativa unites the thought before history (myth) with the thought outside of history (mysticism) in a way that brings the particulars of everyday experience into dialogue with our longing for transcendence. And in the process, it ex-poses the superficiality of all worldly agendas for reform. What troubles modern individuals is the moral insignificance of their lives. Condemned to be free, their freedom sentences them to gratuitous acts of self-assertion. They feel that they must either conquer the world (an impossible task) or die to its values like the saints.

But it is hard to die to the values of this world if there is no convincing alternative to it. And harder still when there has emerged in this world a plethora of tangible pleasures and causes—all claiming our allegiance. But these causes do not survive death, and so they are all ultimately disillusioning. In such a world, Dostoevsky tells us we can live joyfully only until our thirtieth year, sustained like Ivan Karamazov by the "sticky leaves," our desire for desire. After that, distraction, ambition, and vice become life's primary consolations. But if we take a leap into the immaterial world and reeducate our senses to perceive the invisible through the visible, like Blake did, or like Father Zossima, then there is still hope. In fact, this very psychological leap *is* hope—its twentieth-century manifestation.

The contemplative life Merton advocated has nothing to teach us except to reassure us and say that if we dare to pene-trate our own silence and dare to advance without fear into the solitude of our own hearts, and risk sharing that solitude with the lonely other who seeks God through us and with us, "then we will recover the capacity to understand what is be-yond words and beyond explanations and, thereby experience in the depths of our own hearts the intimate union of God's spirit and our own secret inmost self, so that we and He are One Spirit."[11] The goal is to exchange our mind with the mind of Christ. The search for purity of intention that animates the monk's life of prayer turns out to be the engine of authentic social change.

Injustices exist because our concerns are not yet the concerns of God. This is not God's fault but our own, for we haven't yet figured out what God's concerns truly are. We are not, except for a few anticipatory saints among us, actual Beings. Caught up in our individuality, our particularity, our differences, we simply seek the wrong ends.

Merton's insights into the triumph of this illusory self invite us to think against ourselves and our times and to explore the myths that govern our actions and perceptions. Merton did not work in the service to the great society or any other political ideal; he sought nonattachment in order to offer a suprapolitical witness capable of transforming everyday life from the inside out. He was a spokesman for the soul, the deep self, the sublime—a "sign of refusal" to the ways of the world.

The irony of his life was that in turning away from the world, he reentered it from the other side. By refusing the false optimism of the new postwar professional class, he established himself as the premier American outsider in that international cadre of honest souls—George Orwell, Albert Camus, Simone Weil, Arthur Koestler, Boris Pasternak, and Czeslaw Milosz—who bravely stood up at midcentury for the autonomy of the interior life and "the third position of integrity." His influence, like theirs, was profound but largely clandestine, operating in that history within history that contains both the writer's quest for sociophilosophical gnosis and the mystic's search for God.

Merton believed a monk had a duty not to simply survive the modern world but to dissent from it in total transparency of being without affectation, calmly accepting its incomprehension and indifference because what he was living for was so important that the world weighed little in the balance. "In the night of our technological barbarism," Merton wrote, "monks must be as trees which exist silently in the dark and by their vital presence, purify the air."[12]

As a monk, Merton was an apostle, not a genius; a religious man living in a secular Diaspora, who found in the Holy Mother the same thing Yuri Zhivago had found in Lara: a resolute, indefatigable image of the good. And once he had experi-

enced that good, he could no longer conform to the artificial demands of his age nor accept its requisite moral compromises or
spiritual blindness. He was simply too honest and too much
alive to be capable of such treason to himself or to us.

Merton's critics might argue that in taking the long view,
he took too long a view—and in defending the silent self, he
sometimes slighted the outspoken, fallible, compromised, democratic self-in-progress burdened by historical particulars.
And there is an element of truth to this. The Trappist world
view may be radical, but it is not particularly democratic. And
mysticism may open you up to profound states of empathy,
but mystics are notoriously impatient with institutional direc-
tives, committee meetings, and political negotiations.

And yet through the virtue of compassion and the disciplines of prayer, voluntary poverty, and the examination of
conscience, Merton found his way back into solidarity with ordinary people and the poor—recognizing their great dignity
and spiritual longing as his own. And so he began to make his
way up the seven-storey mountain, the purgatory of history,
in his monk's robe. In the process he discovered that it was
not the amount of pain that you endured that propelled your
ascent, but the purity of your intentions. He learned from
Gandhi and King not only that unjust suffering was redemptive but that, when graciously endured, it was also politically
effective. And so he took it upon himself to uphold the
prophetic wing of the contemplative tradition. "Be Here Now,"
that famous sixties' mantra, became for Merton "Be Eternal
Always."

There is no simple way to sum up such a witness. Merton
did not establish a school of prayer nor a new theological system. As a prophet of spiritual longing in a materialistic age,
he provided more questions than answers. And yet through
his Franciscan joy, his Trappist asceticism, his Augustinian
depth, and his transcendental American hope, he offers us all
a vision of the spiritual life unencumbered by rigid philosophical categories, narrow historical agendas, or trite religious
truisms.

Just a few days before he died, Merton had been reading
Nathaniel West's *Miss Lonelyhearts* in Ceylon and copying out

these evocative lines into his journal: "They had run out of seashells and were using faded photographs, soiled fans, time-tables, playing cards, broken toys, imitation jewelry, junk that memory had made precious, far more precious than anything the sea might yield."[13] Such is our improvised spirituality at the end of the century!

But thanks to Thomas Merton we have more than just a few broken toys with which to give shape to our religious aspirations. We have a path of thought leading back through the maze of our discredited spiritual heritage to the Desert Fathers, and further still to the eschatological vision of Christ crucified, resurrected, and redeemed. And if we travel down that path, we may discover the enigma and the enormity of our own souls—just as Merton did—and, by so doing, acquire the courage to live within a reality beyond all predication, a reality that makes plain all the pretenses and perjuries of this world and yet offers us the hope that beyond our small, fictive selves there lies a truer self, a larger identity, a loving God. For Thomas Merton, living a life in accord with that larger reality was living in the light of this faith, and his writings, which describe with great eloquence his own attempts to remain true to this revelation, make up his American Prophecy.

CHRONOLOGY

Early Life

1915   Born January 31 in Prades, France.

1917   Moves to Flushing, New York.

1918   Brother, John Paul, is born.

1921   Mother, Ruth, dies of stomach cancer.

1923   Moves in with his maternal grandparents in Douglaston, Long Island.

1925   Moves with his father to St. Antonin, in Southern France.

1926   Enrolls at the Lycee in Montauban.

1928   Moves with his father, Owen, to the outskirts of London. Enrolls in Ripley Court School.

1929   Enters Oakham Public School in England.

1931   Father dies of a malignant brain tumor.

1933   Visits Italy and the United States, then enters Clare College, Cambridge, in the fall.

1934   Returns to the United States after a desolate year at Cambridge.

1935   Enrolls in Columbia University. Joins the Communist Party. Takes his first course from Mark Van Doren.

1937   Grandfather Samuel Jenkins dies.

Conversion

1938   Graduates from Columbia with a B.A. Enrolls in graduate school for an M.A. in English. Converts to Roman Catholicism.

1939   Receives his M.A. in English from Columbia. Decides to enter the Ph.D. program. Moves to 35 Perry Street in Greenwich Village. That summer moves in with Robert Lax and Edward Rice and writes his novel "The Labyrinth," which was never published. Accepted for admission to the Franciscan Order.

1940   Begins teaching English Composition in the Extension Division of the School of Business at Columbia. Visits Cuba over Easter break. Denied admission to the Franciscans. Takes a job teaching English at St. Bonaventure.

1941   Begins a new novel "The Journal of My Escape from the Nazis." Considers moving to Friendship House in Harlem to work with Baroness de Hueck. Joins the Trappists in Kentucky as a postulant.

1943   Brother John Paul marries. A month later his plane's engines fail over the English channel and he dies at sea.

Holy Orders

1944   Publishes *Thirty Poems* (New Directions) Makes simple vows.

1945   Begins study for the priesthood.

1946   Receives minor orders. Publishes *A Man in the Divided Sea*.

1947   Makes solemn vows: poverty, chastity, and obedience. Publishes "Poetry and the Contemplative Life" in *Commonweal*.

1948   Publishes *The Seven Storey Mountain*, *Guide to Cistercian Life*, *Cistercian Contemplatives*, *Figures for an Apocalypse*, *The Spirit of Simplicity*, *Exile Ends in Glory*. Ordained as subdeacon.

1949   Publishes *Seeds of Contemplation*, *Gethsemani Magnificat*, *The Tears of Blind Lions*, *The Waters of Siloe*, *Elected Silence* (the British edition of *Seven Storey Mountain*). Ordained into the priesthood.

1950   Publishes *Selected Poems, What Are These Wounds*. Treated for colitis.

1951   Becomes Master of Scholastics. Publishes *A Balanced Life of Prayer, The Ascent to Truth*.

1952   Looks into possible transfer to the Carthusian or Camaldolese Orders for greater solitude.

1953   Publishes *The Sign of Jonas, Devotions to Saint John of the Cross, Bread in the Wilderness*.

1954   Publishes *The Last of the Fathers*.

1955   Publishes *No Man Is an Island*. Receives permission to use the forest lookout tower as a hermitage.

1956   Becomes Novice Master at Gethsemani. Incident with the Psychiatrist Zilboorg. Publishes *The Living Bread, Praying the Psalms, Silence in Heaven*.

1957   Publishes *Basic Principles of Monastic Spirituality, The Silent Life, The Strange Islands, The Tower of Babel*. Ernesto Cardenal enters Gethsemani as a novice.

Return to the World

1958   Publishes *Monastic Peace, Thoughts in Solitude, Prometheus: A Meditation, Nativity Kerygma*. Writes to Boris Pasternak and Pope John XXIII.

1959   Publishes *The Christmas Sermons of Blessed Guerric of Igny, The Secular Journal of Thomas Merton, Selected Poems of Thomas Merton*. Writes to D. T. Suzuki. Asks to join Benedictine monastery in Cuernavaca, but is denied permission.

1960   Publishes *The Solitary Life, Spiritual Direction and Meditation, Disputed Questions, The Wisdom of the Desert*. Begins regular visits to the psychologist James Wygal in Louisville. Begins revision of *Seeds of Contemplation*.

1961   Publishes *The Behavior of Titans, The New Man*. Increases correspondence. Begins to address social issues more directly.

1962   Publishes *New Seeds of Contemplation, Original Child Bomb, Hagia Sophia, Clement of Alexandria, Loreto and*

Gethsemani, A Thomas Merton Reader. Told by the abbot general to cease writing material on war and peace. "Prayer for Peace" is read in The House of Representatives by Congressman Frank Kowalski, a democrat from Connecticut. Merton joins the Fellowship of Reconciliation—an antiwar group. Edits *Breakthrough to Peace*—a collection of essays on peace issues (New Directions).

1963   Publishes *Life and Holiness, Breakthrough to Peace, Emblems of a Season of Fury, The Solitary Life, Guigo the Carthusian, Blackfriars*. Publishes "Letters to a White Liberal." Receives the Pax Medal for his writings on nonviolence.

1964   Holds a retreat at Gethsemani on "The Spiritual Roots of Protest" for leaders in the peace movement (sponsored by the Fellowship of Reconciliation: Daniel and Philip Berrigan, A. J. Muste, Jim Forest, Wilbur H. Ferry, John Howard Yoder, John Nelson, Tom Cornel and Tony Walsh). Publishes "Gandhi: The Gentle Revolutionary" in *Ramparts* and *Seeds of Destruction*.

The Hermitage Years

1965   Publishes *Gandhi on Non-Violence, The Way of Chuang Tzu, Seasons of Celebration*. Publishes his first public statement on the war in Vietnam in a letter in *Commonweal*. Begins living permanently in the hermitage on the monastery grounds. Roger La Porte, a Catholic Worker, burns himself to death in front of the United Nations Building in protest against the Vietnam War. Merton temporarily resigns from the Catholic Peace Fellowship.

1966   Publishes *Raids on the Unspeakable, Gethsemani: A Life of Praise, Conjectures of a Guilty Bystander*. Back surgery at St. Joseph's hospital. Begins relationship with student nurse.

1967   Publishes *A Prayer of Cassiodorus*. Arrangements are made for Martin Luther King, Jr., to make a retreat at Gethsemani in Spring 1968.

1968   Publishes four issues of *Monks Pond, Cables to the Ace, Faith and Violence, Zen and the Birds of Appetite*, and the essay "The Vietnam War: An Overwhelming Atrocity" in the *Catholic Worker*. Visits California, New Mexico, and Alaska looking for a possible site for a hermitage. Publishes "Non-Violence Does Not . . . Cannot . . . Mean Passivity" in *Ave Maria*. Gives a series of talks to the Sisters of the Precious Blood (published later as *Thomas Merton in Alaska*) and at The Center for Democratic Studies in Santa Barbara (published later as *Thomas Merton: Preview to the Asian Journey*, edited by Walter Capps). Flies to the far East—visits Calcutta, New Delhi, Madras, Celyon, Singapore, and other cites. Dies in Bangkok of accidental electrocution after delivering a talk "Marxism and Monastic Perspectives" at a meeting of monastic superiors sponsored by the International Benedictine Organization.

Posthumous Publications

1969   *My Argument with the Gestapo, The Geography of Lograire, The True Solitude*

1970   *Opening the Bible, A Hidden Wholeness*

1971   *Contemplation in a World of Action, Thomas Merton on Peace*

1973   *The Asian Journal of Thomas Merton*

1975   *He Is Risen*

1976   *Ishi Means Man*

1977   *The Monastic Journey, The Collected Poems of Thomas Merton*

1978   *A Catch of Anti-Letters* (Thomas Merton and Robert Lax)

1979   *Love and Living*

1980   *Thomas Merton on Saint Bernard, Geography of Holiness, The Nonviolent Alternative*

1981   *The Literary Essays of Thomas Merton, Introductions East and West, Day of a Stranger*

1983   *Woods, Shore, Desert*

1984   Michael Mott publishes the authorized biography *The Seven Mountains of Thomas Merton*

1985   *The Hidden Ground of Love: Letters on Religious Experience and Social Concerns*

1988   *A Vow of Conversation* (journals 1964–65), *Thomas Merton in Alaska*

1989   *The Road to Joy: Letters of Thomas Merton to New and Old Friends*

1990   *The School of Charity: Letters of Thomas Merton on Religious Renewal and Spiritual Direction*

1992   *Thomas Merton: Spiritual Master*

1993   *The Courage for Truth: Letters to Writers*

1994   *Witness to Freedom: The Letters of Thomas Merton in Times of Crisis*

1995   *Run to the Mountain* (journals 1939–41)

1996   *Entering the Silence* (journals 1941–52)

Forthcoming:

Over the next ten years, we will see the publication of still more of Merton's works—most significantly the rest of his journals which, under the general editorship of Brother Patrick Hart, one of Merton's associates at Gethsemani, are expected to run to seven volumes.

Merton's Daily Schedule (circa 1941)*

2:00 A.M.	Rise, go to choir, recite Matins in honor of the Blessed Virgin Mary
2:30 A.M.	Private meditation (kneeling or standing only)
3:00 A.M.	Night Office (canonical Matins and Lauds: chanting of twenty psalms, some canticles, three or twelve lessons, the *Te Deum*, a Gospel reading, and blessing—all in Latin)
4:00 A.M.	Priests say Mass in Latin; others go to Communion
5:00 A.M.	Time for reading or private prayer (Merton sometimes wrote poetry at this time in the early forties)
5:30 A.M.	PRIME: The first of the "Day Hours" supposed to be chanted at dawn—following this schedule the monks would chant all 150 Psalms in the course of a week
6:00 A.M.	Chapter: a kind of business meeting; the abbot often gave a commentary on the Rule of St. Benedict
6:30 A.M.	Coffee and two ounces of dry bread. Reading, study
7:45 A.M.	TIERCE (the "Second Hour" of chants). High Mass
9:00 A.M.	Two hour work period (Merton writes)
10:45 A.M.	Reading or prayer
11:07 A.M.	NONE (the "Fourth Hour")
11:30 A.M.	Dinner (usually potatoes and soup)

*Adapted from *Waters of Siloe* pp. x–xi.

12:15 P.M.	Reading, study, private prayer
1:30 P.M.	Work (more writing and/or physical labor)
3:30 P.M.	Reading or private prayer
4:30 P.M.	Vespers (the most important of the day hours—chanted)
5:15 P.M.	Meditation
5:30 P.M.	Collation (light refreshment)
5:40 P.M.	Reading, study, or private prayer (Merton sometimes slept)
6:10 P.M.	COMPLINE (last of the hours chanted before bed). *Salve Regina* (an antiphon sung in honor of the Virgin Mary). Examination of conscience
7:00 P.M.	Retire

Merton's Daily Schedule
in His Hermitage (1966)*

2:14 A.M.	Rise, lauds, meditation
5:00 A.M.	Breakfast
5:30 A.M.	Prayer, study, and spiritual reading
7:30 A.M.	Prime, then rosary
8:00 A.M.	Manual work, chores etc.
9:30 A.M.	TIERCE
10:30 A.M.	SEXT
11:00 A.M.	NONE
11:30 A.M.	To the monastery for private Mass, thanksgiving, reading from the Psalter, dinner
1:00 P.M.	VESPERS, followed by meditation
2:14 P.M.	Writing, work, or walk
4:15 P.M.	Vigils anticipated
5:00 P.M.	Supper, followed by Compline
6:00 P.M.	New Testament, meditation, examination of conscience
7:00 P.M.	Retire

*Adapted from an unpublished note written by Thomas Merton to Dom James, cited in *Silent Lamp* p. 199.

A MERTON DICTIONARY

"We always have to go back and start from the beginning and make over all the definitions for ourselves again."

—Thomas Merton

Absurdity: "The anguish of realizing that underneath the apparently logical pattern of a more or less 'well organized' and rational life, there lies an abyss of irrationality, confusion, pointlessness, and indeed of apparent chaos. This is what immediately impresses itself upon the man who has renounced diversion. . . . He accepts the difficulty of facing the million things in his life which are incomprehensible instead of simply ignoring them." (DQ 179–80)

Asceticism: "The real purpose of asceticism is not cutting off one's relation to created things and other people, but normalizing and healing it." (HGL 503)

Anxiety: The strain "caused by too complete a dependence on ourselves, on our devices, our own plans, our own idea of what we are able to do." (No Man 224)

Bible: "The central content of the Bible, what it is really about, what opens itself to the amazed understanding of one who really grasps the message, is this unique claim: that the inner truth of man and of human existence is revealed in a certain kind of event. This event has the nature of kairos, crisis, or judgment. Challenged by a direct historical intervention of God (which may be doubtful and obscure but is none the less decisive), man can respond with the engagement

of his deepest freedom, or he can evade the encounter by various spe-
cious excuses. If the encounter is evaded, man's freedom is not vindi-
cated but mortgaged and forfeited. (But the confrontation can be
renewed in other circumstances. One may get another chance!)
When the encounter is real and complete, a new kind of relationship
is established between our own freedom and that ultimate freedom
and spirit; the God who is love and who is also 'Lord of History.' At
the same time a new relationship with other men comes into being:
instead of living for ourselves, we live for them. Ideally speaking, if
we all lived in this kind of altruistic concern and engagement,
human history would culminate in an epiphany of God in man,
mankind would visibly be Christ." (OB 83–84)

Charity: "A love for God which respects the need that other men
have for Him. Therefore, charity alone can give us the power and the
delicacy to love others without defiling their loneliness which is their
need and their salvation." (No Man 244)

Christ: "The Spirit of God must teach us Who Christ is and form
Christ in us and transform us into other Christs. . . . Therefore if you
want to have in your heart the affections and dispositions that were
those of Christ on earth, consult not your own imagination but faith.
Enter into the darkness of interior renunciation, strip your soul of
images and let Christ form Himself in you by His Cross." (NS
156–57)

Conscience: "The light by which we interpret the will of God in our
own lives . . . the summary of the whole man . . . the mirror of a
man's depths . . . the face of the soul . . . buried not only in the invisible recesses of man's own metaphysical secrecy but in the secrecy of
God himself." (No Man 30, 31)

Contemplation: "The highest expression of man's intellectual and
spiritual life. It is that life itself, fully awake, fully active, fully
aware that it is alive. It is spiritual wonder. It is spontaneous awe at
the sacredness of life, of being. It is gratitude for life, for awareness
and for being. It is a vivid realization of the fact that life and being
in us proceed from an invisible, transcendent Source. It is above all
awareness of the reality of that source. It *knows* the Source, obscure-
ly, inexplicably, but with a certitude that goes beyond reason and
beyond simple faith." (NS 1)

"Contemplation does not simply "find" a clear idea of God and confine Him within the limits of that idea, and hold Him there a prisoner to whom it can always return. On the contrary, contemplation is carried away by Him into His own realm. His own mystery and His own freedom. It is pure and virginal knowledge, poor in concepts, poorer still in reasoning, but able, by its very poverty and purity, to follow the Word 'wherever He may go.'" (NS 5)

"It is too close to be explained: it is the intimate union in the depths of your own heart, of God's spirit and your own secret inmost self, so that you and He are in truth One Spirit." (HGL 158)

Contemplative: Someone "who has risked his mind in the desert beyond language and beyond ideas where God is encountered in the nakedness of pure trust, that is to say in the surrender of our poverty and incompleteness in order no longer to clench our minds in a cramp upon themselves, as if thinking made us exist. The message of hope the contemplative offers you, then, brother, is not that you need to find your way through the jungle of language and problems that today surround God, but that whether you understand or not, God loves you, is present in you, lives in you, dwells in you, calls you, saves you, and offers you an understanding and light which are like nothing you ever found in books or heard in sermons." (HGL 158)

Demonic Power: "The objectively evil force (I say objectively with reservations, meaning that it transcends subjective good will), which makes use of and manipulates the best intentions of optimists and turns them to evil, in spite of the hopeful image they have created for themselves: I would call this for want of a better word a demonic force. People ignore it completely because they know that they themselves, want only 'the good.' They do not realize that the good they want is rooted in negation and injustice, that it depends on the vast cruelty of an alientated society that is kept alienated with deliberation." (HGL 318–19)

"It would seem that the a-cultural philistinism of our society (is) the preferred instrument of demonic forces to finally eviscerate all that is left of Christian humanism." (HGL 542)

Despair: "The absolute extreme of self love. It is reached when a man deliberately turns his back on all help from anyone else in order to taste the rotten luxury of knowing himself to be lost . . .

the ultimate development of pride so great and so stiff-necked that it selects the absolute misery of damnation rather than accept happiness from the hands of God and thereby acknowledge that He is above us and that we are not capable of fulfilling our destiny by ourselves. But a man who is truly humble cannot despair, because in the humble man there is no longer any such thing as self-pity." (NS 180)

Detachment: "The habitual disposition of one who is not enslaved by the appetites and necessities of human nature. While remaining subject to the limitations and needs of a human body and soul, the man who is 'detached' is not dominated by the desire of pleasure or the fear of pain; his will is able to function freely without being dominated by self-interest. The acquisition of detachment is the proximate end of all asceticism. Christian detachment is distinguished by its supernatural character. It is ordered not merely to the perfection of the individual but to the love and service of God and, ultimately, to union with God in contemplation." (WOS 361–62)

Education: "Showing a person how to define himself authentically and spontaneously in relation to his world—not to impose a prefabricated definition of the world, still less an arbitrary definition of the individual himself. . . . Learning who one is, and learning what one has to offer the contemporary world, and then learning how to make that offering valid." (Love and Living 3)

"We must provide an education that strengthens us against the noise, the violence, and the half-truths of our materialistic society." (DQ 148)

Eschatology: "Eschatology is not *finis* and punishment, the winding up of accounts and the closing of books: it is the final beginning, the definitive birth into a new creation. It is not the last gasp of exhausted possibilities but the first taste of all that is beyond conceiving as actual." (Raids 75)

Existentialism: "An experience and an attitude, rather than a system of thought. As soon as it begins to present itself as a system, it denies and destroys itself. Non-objective, elusive, concrete, dynamic, always in movement and always seeking to renew itself in the newness of the present situation, genuine existentialism is, like Zen

Buddhism and like apophatic Christian mysticism, hidden in life itself. It cannot be distilled our in verbal formulas." (MZ 258)

"Pragmatism and positivism are . . . interested in the question *how*. Traditional metaphysics, whether scholastic (realist) or idealist, is interested in the question *what* (the essence). Existentialism wants to know *who*. It is interested in the authentic use of freedom by the concrete personal subject." (MZ 263).

Faith: "Primarily intellectual assent. But if it were only that and nothing more, if it were only the 'argument of what does not appear,' it would not be complete. . . . It is also a grasp, a contact, a communion of wills, the substance of things hoped for. . . . One says 'yes' not merely to a statement *about* God, but to the Invisible, Infinite God Himself. . . . Faith then is not just the grim determination to cling to a certain form of words, no matter what may happen—though we must certainly be prepared to defend our creed with our life. But above all faith is the opening of the inward eye, the eye of the heart, to be filled with the presence of the Divine light." (NS 128–30)

"Faith means doubt. Faith is not the suppression of doubt. It is the overcoming of doubt, and you overcome doubt by going through it. The man of faith who has never experienced doubt is not a man of faith. Consequently, the monk is one who has to struggle in the depths of his being with the presence of doubt, and to go through what some religions call the Great Doubt, to break through beyond doubt into a servitude which is very, very deep because it is not his own personal servitude, it is the servitude of God Himself, in us." (SM 228)

Freedom: "The ability to do the will of God." (NS 201)

God: "The God Who is God and not a philosopher's abstraction, lies infinitely beyond the reach of anything our eyes can see or our minds can understand. No matter what perfection you predicate of Him, you have to add that your concept is only a pale analogy of the perfection that is in God, and that He is not literally what you conceive by that term." (NS 131)

Gospel: "The news that, if I will, I can respond now in perfect freedom to the redemptive love of God for man in Christ, that I can *now* rise above the forces of necessity and evil in order to say 'yes' to the mysterious action of Spirit that is transforming the world even in the midst of the violence and confusion and destruction that seem to proclaim His absence and His 'death.'" (CGB 113)

Hell: "Where no one has anything in common with anybody else except the fact that they all hate one another and cannot get away from one another and from themselves. . . . And the reason why they want to be free from one another is not so much that they hate what they see in others, as that they know others hate what they see in them; and all recognize in one another what they detest in themselves: selfishness and impotence, agony, terror and despair." (NS 123)

Hope: "The living heart of asceticism. It teaches us to deny ourselves and leave the world not because we or the world are evil, but because unless a supernatural hope raises us above the things of time we are in no condition to make a perfect use of our own or of the world's true goodness." (No Man 18, 19).

"We are not perfectly free until we live in pure hope. . . . Hope empties our hands in order that we may work with them. It shows us that we have something to work for, and teaches us how to work for it." (No Man 14, 15)

Humility: "A virtue, not a neurosis . . . sets us free to do what is really good, by showing us our *illusions* and withdrawing our will from what was only an *apparent* good." (TIS 65)

"Humility and consolation go together, for humility is truth experienced in its concrete and existential factuality in our own life. One who simply 'runs his own life' by putting into effect ideal projects designed to establish his own ego-image more and more firmly cannot possibly take consolation from God. He is not debarred from consolations—those which come from the image he has constructed for himself! But these consolations are laborious fabrications ambivalent and nauseating to anyone with a sense of truth." (CIWA 286)

Idolatry: "Servitude to human systems that exploit man's natural needs and appetites for their own ends, or seek to dominate him by brute force." (OB 48)

"Idols dominate specific areas of life from outside it, because they are in fact projections of man's fragmented desires and projections. It is the idols that man goes out to meet when he reaches his own limit, and they are called to supplement his strength and his ingenuity when these run out." (OB 65)

Infused Prayer: "The term *infused*, applied to prayer, contemplation, knowledge, love, etc., is generally synonymous with 'mystical,' and signifies an effect that is directly produced in the soul by God without active intervention on the part of the soul, which is moved passively to a knowledge or love of God completely transcending all the faculties of human nature. However, when speaking of 'infused' virtues, whether moral or theological, Catholic writers use the term in a broader sense, to signify habits produced in the soul by God gratuitously, since they are supernatural, but in which the active cooperation of the soul plays an influential part." (WOS 363)

Liberty: "A talent given us by God, an instrument to work with. It is the tool with which we build our own lives, our own happiness. Our true liberty is something we must never sacrifice, for if we sacrifice it we renounce God Himself. Only the false spontaneity of caprice, the pseudo liberty of sin is to be sacrificed. Our true liberty must be defended with life itself for it's the most precious element in our being. It is our liberty that makes us Persons, constituted in the divine image. The supernatural society of the Church has, as one of its chief functions, the preservation of our spiritual liberty as sons of God. How few people realize this!" (NS 202)

Meditation: "A twofold discipline that has a twofold function. First it is supposed to give you sufficient control over your mind and memory and will to enable you to recollect yourself and withdraw from exterior things . . . and second—this is the real end of meditation—it teaches you how to become aware of the presence of God; and most of all it aims at bringing you to a state of almost constant loving attention to God, and dependence on Him." (NS 217)

"If you succeed in emptying your mind of every thought and every desire, you may indeed withdraw into the center of yourself and concentrate everything within you upon the imaginary point where your life springs out of God: you will not really find God. No natural exercise can bring you into vital contact with Him. Unless He utters Himself in you, speaks His own name in the center of your soul, you will no more know Him than a stone knows the ground upon which it rests in its inertia." (NS 39)

Monastery: "A school in which we learn from God how to be happy." (SSM 372)

It is "an earthly paradise because it is an earthly purgatory." (SJ 186)

Monk: "The monk is a Christian who has responded to a special call from God, and has withdrawn from the more active concerns of worldly life, in order to devote himself completely to repentance, conversion, *metanoia*, renunciation and prayer. In positive terms, we must understand the monastic life above all as a life of prayer. The negative elements, solitude, fasting obedience, penance, renunciation of property and of ambition, are all intended to clear the way so that prayer, meditation, and contemplation may fill the space created by the abandonment of other concerns." (CP 19)

"The monk is a man who completely renounces the familiar patterns of human and social life and follows the call of God into 'the desert' or 'the wilderness' that is to say, into the land that is unknown to him and unfrequented by other men. His journey into the wilderness is not a mere evasion from the world and its responsibilities. Negative reasons cannot adequately account for the monastic journey into solitude. Monastic renunciation is the answer to a positive call from God, inexplicable, not subject to scientific demonstration, yet able to be verified by faith and the spiritual wisdom of the Church." (MJ 16)

"(The monk) is a man who has been called by the Holy Spirit to relinquish the cares, desires and ambitions of other men, and devote his entire life to seeking God. The concept is familiar. The reality which the concepts signifies is a mystery. For in actual fact, no one on earth knows precisely what it means to seek God until he himself has set out to find Him. No man can tell another what his search means unless that other is enlightened, at the same time, by the Spirit speaking within his own heart. In the end, no one can seek God unless he has already begun to find Him. No one can find God without having first been found by Him. A monk is a man who seeks God because he has been found by God." (SL vii)

Mortification. "The virtue by which we 'mortify'—that is 'put to death'—the rebellious desires and appetites of our soul in order to liberate our potentialities for good, that they may be elevated to high perfection by the action of God's efficacious grace." (WOS 364)

Mysticism: "A way of prayer, or of contemplation, or simply of living, in which the direct action and influence of God tend to dominate and absorb the activity of our natural faculties, raising them to a habitually supernatural level. The characteristic external mark of true Christian mysticism is not a succession of flamboyant experiences and phenomena, but a life of constant peace, recollection, absorption in God, charity, humility and, last but not least, balance and common sense, even in the midst of great trials, distracting duties, or heroic suffering." (WOS 364)

Nonviolence: "The most exacting of all forms of struggle not only because it demands first of all that one be ready to suffer evil and even face the threat of death without violent retaliation, but because it excludes mere transient self-interest, even political, from its considerations. In a very real sense, he who practices non-violent resistance must commit himself not to the defense of his own interests or even those of a particular group: he must commit himself to the defense of objective truth and right and above all of *man*. . . . He is fighting for everybody." (FAV 14, 15)

Person: "A person is a person insofar as he has a secret and is a solitude of his own that cannot be communicated to anyone else. If I love a person, I will love that which most makes him a person: the secrecy, the hiddenness, the solitude of his own individual being, which God alone can penetrate and understand." (No Man 244, 245)

Personalism: "Gives priority to the person and not the individual self. To give priority to the person means respecting the unique and inalienable value of the other person, as well as one's own, for a respect that is centered only on one's individual self to the exclusion of others proves itself fraudulent." (WCT 17)

Poetry: "The flowering of ordinary possibilities . . . the fulfillment of all the momentous predictions hidden in everyday life." (Literary Essays 373)

Priest: Someone whose task is "to spiritualize the world." (SOJ 301)

Prayer: "Freedom and affirmation growing out of nothingness into love. Prayer is the flowering of our inmost freedom, in response to the Word of God. Prayer is not only dialogue with God: it is the communion of our freedom with His ultimate freedom, His infinite spirit. It is the elevation of our limited freedom into the infinite freedom of the divine spirit, and of divine love. Prayer is the encounter of our freedom with the all embracing charity which knows no limit and knows no obstacle. Prayer is an emergence into this area of infinite freedom." (CIWA 333)

"The whole function of the life of prayer is . . . to enlighten and strengthen our conscience so that it not only knows and perceives the outward, written precepts of the moral and divine laws, but above all lives God's law in concrete reality by perfect and continual union with His will. The conscience that is united to the Holy Spirit by faith, hope, and selfless charity becomes a mirror of God's own interior law which is His charity." (No Man 41)

Prophecy: "Not to predict, but to seize upon reality in its moment of highest expectation and tension toward the new." (Literary Essays 373)

Prophet: Someone "whose whole life is a living witness of the providential action of God in the world." (SOJ 11)

Purity of Heart: "An unconditional and totally humble surrender to God, a total acceptance of ourselves and of our situation as willed by him. It means the renunciation of all deluded images of ourselves, all exaggerated estimates of our capacities in order to obey God's will . . . the 'self' as recognized in the context of realities willed by God . . . the enlightened awareness of the new man as opposed to the complex and perhaps rather disreputable fantasies of the old man" (CP 68).

"A clear unobstructed vision of the true state of affairs, an intuitive grasp of one's own inner reality as anchored, or rather lost, in God through Christ. The fruit of this is quiet: rest . . . sanity and poise of being that no longer has to look at itself because it is carried away by the perfection of freedom that is in it." (WD 8)

"(Eckhart) admits that: 'To be a proper abode for God and fit for God to act in, a man should also be free from all things and actions, both inwardly and outwardly.' This is Cassian's 'purity of heart' and it corresponds to the idea of 'spiritual virginity' in some Christian mystics. But now Eckhart goes on to say that there is much more: 'A man should be so poor that he is not and has not a place for God to act in. To perceive a place would be to maintain distinctions.' 'A man should be so disinterested and untrammeled that he does not know what God is doing in him.'" (Birds 9)

Reading: "An act of homage to the God of all truth. We open our hearts to words that reflect the reality He has created or the greater Reality which he is. It is also an act of humility and reverence towards other men who are the instruments by which God communicated His truth to us." (TIS 62)

Recollection: "A change of spiritual focus and an attuning of our whole soul to what is beyond and above ourselves. It is a 'conversion' or a 'turning' of our being to spiritual things and to God. And because spiritual things are simple, recollection is also at the same time a simplification of our state of mind and of our spiritual activity. It purifies our intention." (No Man 217)

Sainthood: "A saint is a sign from God. His life bears witness to God's fidelity to promises made to man from the beginning. He tells us who God is by fulfilling God's promises in himself and by being *full of God*." (DQ 274)

"For me to be a saint means to be myself. Therefore the problem of sanctity and salvation is in fact the problem of finding out who I am and discovering my true self." (NS 31)

"The saints are what they are, not because their sanctity makes them admirable to others, but because the gift of sainthood makes it possible for them to admire everybody else." (NS 57)

Self (False): "The man I want myself to be but who cannot exist, because God does not know anything about him. . . . The one who wants to exist outside the reach of God's will and God's love—outside of reality and outside of life . . . an illusion. For most people in the world there is no greater subjective reality than this false self of theirs, which cannot exist. A life devoted to the cult of this shadow is what is called a life of sin." (NS 34)

Self (Real): "At the center of our being is a point of nothingness which is untouched by sin and by illusion, a point of pure truth, a point or spark which belongs entirely to God, which is never at our disposal, from which God disposes of our lives, which is inaccessible to the fantasies of our own mind or the brutalities of our own will.

This little point of nothingness and of absolute poverty is the pure glory of God in us. It is so to speak His name written in us, as poverty, as our indigence, as our dependence, as our sonship. It is like a pure diamond, blazing with the invisible light of heaven. It is in everybody. . . . I have no program for this seeing. It is only given. But the gate of heaven is everywhere." (CGB 142)

Sincerity: "A divine gift, a clarity of spirit that comes only with grace. . . . Sincerity must be bought at a price: the humility to recognize our innumerable errors, and fidelity in tirelessly setting them right. The sincere man, therefore, is one who has the grace to know that he may be instinctively insincere, and that even his natural sincerity may become a camouflage for irresponsibility and moral cowardice: as if it were enough to recognize the truth, and do nothing about it!" (No Man 192–93)

Solitary: "One who is called to make one of the most terrible decisions possible to man: the decision to disagree completely with those who imagine that the call to diversion and self-deception is the voice of truth and who can summon the full authority of their own prejudice to prove it. He is therefore bound to sweat blood in anguish, in order to be loyal to God, to the Mystical Christ, and to humanity as a whole, rather than to the idol which is offered to him, for his homage by a particular group. He must renounce the blessing of every convenient illusion that absolves him from responsibility when he is untrue to his deepest self and his inmost truth—the image of God in his own soul." (DQ 183)

Solitude: "Not merely the absence of people. True solitude is a participation in the solitariness of God—Who is in all things. His solitude is not a local absence but a metaphysical transcendence. His solitude is His Being. For us, solitude is not a matter of being something *more* than other men, except by accident; for those who cannot be alone cannot find their true being and they are always something less than themselves. For us solitude means withdrawal from an artificial and fictional level of being which men, divided by original sin, have fabricated in order to keep peace with concupiscence and death. But by that very fact the solitary finds himself on the level of a more perfect spiritual society—the city of those who have become real enough to confess and glorify God (that is: life), in the teeth of death." (SOJ 269)

"A false solitude is a point of vantage from which an individual, who has been denied the right to become a person, takes revenge on society by turning his individuality into a destructive weapon. True solitude is found in humility, which is infinitely rich. False solitude is the refuge of pride, and it is infinitely poor. The poverty of false solitude comes from an illusion which pretends, by adorning itself in things it can never possess, to distinguish one individual self from the mass of other men. True solitude is selfless. Therefore, it is rich in silence and charity and peace . . . it cleans the soul, lays it wide open to the four winds of generosity." (No Man 247–48)

Spiritual Direction: "A continuous process of formation and guidance, in which a Christian is led and encouraged *in his special vocation*, so that by faithful correspondence to the graces of the Holy Spirit he may attain to the particular end of his vocation and to union with God." (SD 14–15)

Symbolism: "Expresses and encourages man's acceptance of his own center, his own ontological roots in a mystery that transcends his individual ego." (LL 57)

"Opens the way to an intuitive understanding of mystery—it places us in the presence of the invisible." (DQ 265)

Theology: "The act of the believing person reflecting upon his belief and studying it methodically in order to reach a deeper understanding of God's revelation and to surrender himself more fully and more intelligently to God's manifest will and plan of salvation in the contemporary world." (LL 92)

Truth: "Truth, in things, is their reality. In our minds, it is the conformity of our knowledge with the things known. In our words it is the conformity of our words to what we think. In our conduct, it is the conformity of our acts to what we are supposed to be." (Reader 120–21)

Vocation: "Our vocation is not simply to *be*, but to work together with God in the creation of our own life, our own identity, our own destiny . . . actively participate in His creative freedom, in our own lives, and in the lives of others, by choosing the truth. To put it better, we are even called to share with God the work of creating the truth of our identity." (NS 32)

Wisdom: "The knowledge of Truth in its inmost reality, the experience of Truth arrived at through the rectitude of our own soul. Wisdom knows God in ourselves and ourselves in God. The fear which is the first step to wisdom is the fear of being untrue to God and to ourselves, that we have thrown down our lives at the feet of a false god." (TIS 82)

World: "The way to find the real 'world' is not merely to measure and observe what is outside us, but to discover our own inner ground. For that is where the world is, first of all: in my deepest self. . . . This 'ground,' this 'world,' where I am mysteriously present at once to my own self and to the freedoms of all other men, is not a visible, objective and determined structure with fixed laws and demands. It is a living and self-creating mystery of which I am myself a part, to which I am myself my own unique door." (CIWA 154–55)

Worldliness: "The involvement in the massive and absurd mythology of technological culture and in all the contrived and obsessive gyrations of its empty mind. One of the symptoms of this is precisely the anguished concern to keep up with an ever-changing, complex, and fictitious orthodoxy in taste, in politics, in cult, in belief, in theology and what not, cultivation of the ability to redefine one's identity day by day in concert with the self-definition of society. 'Worldliness' in my mind is typified by this kind of servitude to care and to illusion, this agitation about thinking the right thoughts and wearing the right hats, this crude and shameful concern not with truth but only with vogue. To my mind, the concern of Christians to be in fashion lest they 'lose the world' is only another pitiable admission that they have lost it." (CGB 259–60)

Zen: Spiritual practice "that rejects all systematic elaborations in order to get back, as far as possible, to the pure unarticulated and unexplained ground of direct experience." (Birds 36)
"The practice of Zen aims at deepening, purification, and transformation of consciousness. But it does not rest satisfied with any 'deepening' or a superficial 'purification.' It seeks the most radical transformation: it works on depths that would seem to go beyond even depth psychology. It has, in other words, a metaphysical and spiritual dimension. It seeks the pure ontological subject, at once unique and universal, no longer 'individual.'" (MZ 238)

"The whole aim of Zen is not to make foolproof statements about experience, but to come to direct grips with reality without the mediation of logical verbalizing. . . . The Zen experience is a direct grasp of the *unity* of the invisible and the visible, the noumenal and the phenomenal, or, if you prefer, an experiential realization that any such division is bound to be pure imagination." (SM 403)

WORKS CITED IN THE MERTON DICTIONARY

"While I'm very happy that I did know him, I always felt the deeper part of Merton he revealed only in his books".

—Abbot Flavian Burns

(AJ) *The Asian Journal of Thomas Merton.* Ed. Naomi Burton, Brother Patrick Hart, and James Laughlin (New York: New Directions, 1973).

(BT) *The Behavior of Titans* (New York: New Directions, 1961).

(Birds) *Zen and the Birds of Appetite* (New York: New Directions, 1968).

(CP) *The Collected Poems of Thomas Merton*, (New York: New Directions, 1977).

(CGB) *Conjectures of a Guilty Bystander* (Garden City, N.Y.: Doubleday, 1966).

(CIWA) *Contemplation in a World of Action* (Garden City, N.Y.: Doubleday, 1971).

(CP) *Contemplative Prayer* (Garden City, N.Y.: Doubleday, 1971).

(CFT) *Courage for Truth.* Ed. Christine M. Bochen (New York: Farrar, Straus, Giroux, 1993).

(DQ) *Disputed Questions* (New York: Harcourt, Brace, Jovanovich, 1960).

(FAV) *Faith and Violence: Christian Teaching and Christian Practice*, (Notre Dame, Ind.: University of Notre Dame Press, 1968).

(HGL) *The Hidden Ground of Love: Letters on Religious Experience and Social Concerns*. Ed. William H. Shannon (New York: Harcourt, Brace, Jovanovich, 1985).

(HR) *"Honorable Reader" Reflections on My Work*. Ed. Robert Daggy (New York: Crossroads, 1989).

(Ishi) *Ishi Means Man* (Greensboro, N.C.: Unicorn, 1976).

(Literary Essays) *The Literary Essays of Thomas Merton*. Ed. Brother Patrick Hart (New York: New Directions, 1981).

(LL) *Love and Living*. Ed. Naomi Burton Stone and Brother Patrick Hart (New York: Farrar, Straus, Giroux, 1979).

(MAG) *My Argument with the Gestapo* (Garden City, N.Y.: Doubleday, 1969).

(MJ) *The Monastic Journey*. Ed. Brother Patrick Hart (Garden City, N.Y.: Doubleday, 1978).

(MZ) *Mystics and Zen Masters* (New York: Farrar, Straus, Giroux, 1967).

(No Man) *No Man Is an Island* (New York: Harcourt, Brace, Jovanovich, 1955).

(NS) *New Seeds of Contemplation* (New York: New Directions, 1962).

(NVA) *The Nonviolent Alternative*. Ed. Gordon C. Zahn (New York: Farrar, Straus, Giroux, 1980). Originally published under the title *Thomas Merton on Peace* in 1971.

(OB) *Opening the Bible* (Collegeville, Minn.: Liturgical Press, 1970).

(Raids) *Raids on the Unspeakable* (New York: New Directions, 1966).

(Reader) *A Thomas Merton Reader*. Ed. Thomas P. McDonnell (Garden City, N.Y.: Doubleday, 1974).

(SD) *Spiritual Direction and Meditation* (Hertfordshire, England: Anthony Clarke, 1975).

(SJ) *The Secular Journal of Thomas Merton* (New York: Farrar, Straus, Giroux, 1959).

(SL) *The Silent Life* (New York: Farrar, Straus, Giroux, 1957).

(SM) *Thomas Merton: Spiritual Master*. Ed. Lawrence Cunningham (New York: Paulist Press, 1992).

(SOD) *Seeds of Destruction*, (New York, Farrar, Straus, Giroux, 1964).

(SOJ) *Sign of Jonas* (New York: Harcourt, Brace, Jovanovich, 1953).

(Springs) *The Springs of Contemplation.* Ed. Jane Marie Richardson (New York: Farrar, Straus, Giroux, 1992).

(SSM) *The Seven Storey Mountain* (New York: Harcourt, Brace, Jovanovich, 1948).

(TIS) *Thoughts in Solitude* (New York: Farrar, Straus, Giroux, 1958).

(V) *Vow of Conversation: Diary: 1964–1965.* Ed. Naomi Burton Stone (New York: Farrar, Straus, Giroux, 1988).

(WCT) *The Way of Chuang-Tzu* (New York: New Directions, 1965).

(WD) *The Wisdom of the Desert: Sayings from the Desert Fathers of the Fourth Century.* Trans. Thomas Merton (New York: New Directions, 1960).

(WOS) *The Waters of Siloe* (New York: Harcourt, Brace, Jovanorich, 1949).

NOTES

Introduction

1. Kierkegaard, Søren, *The Present Age*, trans. Alexander Dru (San Francisco: Harper and Row, 1962), p. 105.

2. Interview with Jean Jadot in *Merton by Those Who Knew Him Best*, ed. Paul Wilkes (San Francisco: Harper and Row, 1984).

3. Interview with W. H. Ping Ferry in *Merton by Those Who Knew Him Best*.

4. Merton, Thomas, *"Honorable Reader" Reflections on My Work*, ed. Robert Daggy (New York: Crossroads, 1989), p. 67.

Chapter One: Early Life

1. Merton, Thomas, *The Seven Storey Mountain* (New York: Harcourt, Brace, Jovanovich, 1948), p. 3.

2. *Seven Storey Mountain*, p. 51.

3. Mott, Michael, *The Seven Mountains of Thomas Merton* (Boston: Houghton Mifflin, 1984), p. 65.

4. Mott, p. 62.

5. *Seven Storey Mountain*, p. 143.

6. *Seven Storey Mountain*, p. 135.

7. *Seven Storey Mountain*, pp. 140–41.

8. Mott, p. 98.

9. Emerson, Ralph Waldo, "The American Scholar," in *The Literature of the United States*, Vol. 1, 3d ed. Ed. Walter Blair et al. (Glenview, Ill.: Scott, Foresman, 1971), p. 1076.

Chapter Two: Conversion

1. *Seven Storey Mountain*, p. 175.

2. Robert Lax has published several volumes of poetry. He now lives on the island of Patmos in Greece. He went to Columbia with Merton, lived with him during the summer breaks, and remained one of his closest friends throughout his life. His publications include *The Circus of the Sun* (New York: Journeyman Books, 1960); *A Poem for Thomas Merton* (New York: Journeyman Books, 1969); *A Catch of Anti-Letters* with Thomas Merton, foreword by Patrick Hart (Mission, KS: Sheed, Andrews & McNeal, 1978); *Dark Earth / Night Sky* (New York: Journeyman Books, 1985); and *33 Poems* (New York: New Directions, 1988).

3. Mott, p. 109 (see Ch. 1, n. 3).

4. *Seven Storey Mountain*, p. 199.

5. *Seven Storey Mountain*, p. 203.

6. *Seven Storey Mountain*, p. 204.

7. *Seven Storey Mountain*, p. 205.

8. Merton, Thomas, *No Man Is an Island* (New York: Harcourt, Brace, Jovanovich, 1955), pp. 41–42.

9. The best single, sustained consideration of Merton's take on this distinction between the false self and the real self is James Finley's *Merton's Palace of Nowhere* (Notre Dame, Ind.: Ave Maria Press, 1978).

10. *Seven Storey Mountain*, p. 237.

11. *Seven Storey Mountain*, p. 237–38.

12. *A Thomas Merton Reader*, ed. Thomas P. McDonnell (Garden City, N.Y.: Doubleday, 1974), p. 125.

13. *Seven Storey Mountain*, p. 237.

14. *Seven Storey Mountain*, p. 253.

15. *The Secular Journal of Thomas Merton* (New York: Farrar, Straus, Giroux, 1959), p. 98.

16. *The Secular Journal*, pp. 183–84.

17. *My Argument with the Gestapo* (Garden City, N.Y.: Doubleday, 1969), p. 52.

18. *My Argument with the Gestapo*, pp. 52–53.

19. *My Argument with the Gestapo*, pp. 55–56.

20. Shannon, William H., *Silent Lamp: The Thomas Merton Story* (New York: Crossroads, 1992), p. 101.

21. *Seven Storey Mountain*, p. 355.

22. *Seven Storey Mountain*, p. 362.

23. *The Secular Journal*, p. 270.

Chapter Three: The Monastic Turn

1. *Seven Storey Mountain*, p. 423.

2. See "The Adversary Culture and the New Class," in *The Bloody Crossroads: Where Literature and Politics Meet* (New York: Simon and Schuster, 1986), p. 115.

3. Mott, pp. 208–09 (see Ch. 1, n. 3).

4. Merton, Thomas, *The Waters of Siloe* (New York: Harcourt, Brace, Jovanovich, 1949), pp. x–xi.

5. Mott, p. 214.

6. Pennington, M. Basil, O.C.S.O., *Thomas Merton, Brother Monk: The Quest for True Freedom* (San Francisco: Harper and Row, 1987), p. 3.

7. Mott, pp. 218–19.

8. Mott, p. 215.

9. *Seven Storey Mountain*, pp. 383–84.

10. *"Honorable Reader" Reflections on My Work*, ed. Robert Daggy (N.Y.: Crossroads, 1989); p. 65.

11. Daggy, p. 65.

12. Mott, p. 205.

13. *Seven Storey Mountain*, pp. 389–90.

14. *Seven Storey Mountain*, p. 402.

15. *Seven Storey Mountain*, p. 404.

16. *The Collected Poems of Thomas Merton* (New York: New Directions, 1977), p. 81.

17. *Collected Poems*, p. 167.

18. *Collected Poems*, p. 181.

19. Mott, p. 242.

20. *Sign of Jonas* (New York: Harcourt, Brace, Jovanovich, 1953), p. 40.

21. Mott, p. 226.

22. Mott, p. 227.

Chapter Four: The Seven Storey Mountain

1. *Seven Storey Mountain*, p. 169.

2. *Seven Storey Mountain*, p. 407.

3. Kripalani, Krishna ed., *All Men Are Brothers* (Almedabad, India: Navajivan, 1960), p. 83.

4. Quoted in Cooper, David D., *Thomas Merton's Art of Denial: The Evolution of a Radical Humanist* (Athens and London: University of Georgia Press, 1989), pp. 139–40.

5. Shannon, William H., ed., *The Hidden Ground of Love: Letters on Religious Experience and Social Concerns* (New York: Harcourt, Brace, Jovanovich, 1985), p. 309.

Chapter Five: New Seeds of Contemplation

1. Merton, Thomas, *New Seeds of Contemplation* (New York: New Directions, 1962), p. xii.

2. *New Seeds*, p. 187.

3. I go into this in greater detail in my essay "Gandhi: Non-violence as Poetic Making" in *The Ignorant Perfection of Ordinary People* (Albany: State University of New York Press, 1991).

4. Fox, Richard, *Reinhold Niebuhr: A Biography* (New York: Pantheon, 1985), p. 295.

Chapter Six: Merton as Educator

1. *Sign of Jonas*, p. 330.

2. Merton, Thomas, *Contemplation in a World of Action* (Garden City, N.Y.: Doubleday, 1971), p. 281.

3. *New Seeds*, p. 271.

4. *Contemplation in a World of Action*, p. 280.

5. Finley, James, *Merton's Palace of Nowhere* (Notre Dame, Ind.: Ave Maria Press, 1978), p. 111.

6. Merton, Thomas, *Love and Living*, ed. Naomi Burton Stone and Brother Patrick Hart (New York: Farrar, Straus, Giroux, 1979), p. 9.

7. Pennington, p. 109 (see Ch. 3, n. 6).

8. Griffin, John Howard, *Follow the Ecstasy: Thomas Merton—The Hermitage Years 1965–1968* (Fort Worth: JHG Editions/Latitudes Press, 1983), p. 201.

9. *New Seeds*, p. 34.

10. *New Seeds*, p. 34.

11. Merton, Thomas, *Thoughts in Solitude* (New York: Farrar, Straus, Giroux, 1958), p. 16.

12. Mott, p. 275 (see Ch. 1, n. 3).

13. *Sign of Jonas*, pp. 8–9.

14. *Thoughts in Solitude*, p. 89.

15. *Love and Living*, p. 10.

16. *Love and Living*, pp. 10–11.

Chapter Seven: Toward a Politics of Being

1. Shannon, p. 309, (see Ch. 4, n. 5).

2. Shannon, p. 159.

3. Merton, Thomas, *Disputed Questions* (New York: Harcourt, Brace, Jovanovich, 1960), p. 190.

4. *A Thomas Merton Reader*, p. 506.

5. *No Man Is an Island*, pp. 125–26.

6. Merton, Thomas, *Conjectures of a Guilty Bystander* (Garden City, N.Y.: Doubleday, 1966), pp. 216–17.

7. *Contemplation in a World of Action*, pp. 334–84.

8. Merton, Thomas, *Faith and Violence: Christian Teaching and Christian Practice*, (Notre Dame, Ind.: University of Notre Dame Press, 1968), p. 150.

9. Merton, Thomas, *A Search for Solitude* (San Francisco: Harper & Row, 1996) p. 211.

Chapter Eight: Second Calling

1. *Conjectures of a Guilty Bystander*, pp. 140–41.

2. *Disputed Questions*, pp. x–xi.

3. *Disputed Questions*, p. 13.

4. *Disputed Questions*, p. 18.

5. For a full explanation of Merton's use of this "ecological" metaphor see his letter to B. Hubbard in *Witness to Freedom* (New York: Farrar, Straus, Giroux, 1994).

6. Shannon, pp. 482–83 (see Ch. 4, n. 5).

7. This essay—"Thomas Merton and the Tradition of American Critical Romanticism"—can be found in the anthology *The Message of Thomas Merton*, edited by Brother Patrick Hart and published by Cistercian Publications in 1981 (Kalamazoo, Michigan), p. 166.

8. Letter to the author, December 13, 1994.

9. Merton, Thomas, *The Way of Chuang-Tzu* (New York: New Directions, 1965), pp. 42–43.

10. *Conjectures of a Guilty Bystander*, p. 55.

Chapter Nine: Prometheus Reconsidered

1. *A Thomas Merton Reader*, p. 182.

2. *The Seven Storey Mountain*, p. 341.

3. It is fitting that Mailer's protagonist Sam Slovoda puts himself to sleep using an autohypnosis technique gleaned from a book on Zen Buddhism—a technique, by the way, that Merton mentions in *The Seven Storey Mountain* (p. 187) as the only practical thing he got out his first readings of the Asian spiritual masters.

4. David Noble, *The American Adam in the New World Garden: The Central Myth in the American Novel Since 1830* (New York: George Braziller, 1968), p. 206.

5. Merton, Thomas, *Raids on the Unspeakable* (New York: New Directions, 1966), pp. 87–88.

6. *Thoughts in Solitude*, p. 22.

7. *Thoughts in Solitude*, pp. 66–67.

8. *Love and Living*, pp. 36–37.

Chapter Ten: The Third Position of Integrity

1. *Courage for Truth*, ed. Christine M. Bochen (New York: Farrar, Straus, Giroux, 1993), pp. 54–55.

2. *Thomas Merton: Preview to the Asian Journey*, edited with introduction by Walter Capps (New York: Crossroads, 1989), pp. 69–70.

3. Merton, Thomas, "The Inner Experience," reprinted in *Thomas Merton: Spiritual Master*, ed. Lawrence Cunningham (New York: Paulist Press, 1992), p. 341.

4. *Disputed Questions*, p. 160.

5. King, Coretta Scott, ed., *The Words of Martin Luther King* (New York: Newmarket Press, 1984), p. 74.

6. Shannon, p. 136 (see Ch. 4, n. 5).

7. *A Thomas Merton Reader*, p. 279.

8. Quoted in Forest, Jim, *Living in Wisdom: A Life of Thomas Merton* (Maryknoll, N.Y.: Orbis, 1991), p. 9.

9. Merton, Thomas, *Seeds of Destruction* (New York: Farrar, Straus, Giroux, 1964), p. 14.

10. See Martin Marty, "To: Thomas Merton, Re: Your Prophecy," *National Catholic Reporter* 3, (Aug. 30, 1967): 6.

11. Shannon, *Hidden Ground of Love*, p. 272.

12. Mott, p. 375 (see Ch. 1, n. 3).

13. *Collected Poems*, p. 345.

14. *Collected Poems*, p. 349.

Chapter Eleven: The Mystic as Public Intellectual

1. Huxley, Aldous, *Ends and Means: An Inquiry into the Nature of Ideals and into the Methods Employed for Their Realization* (New York: Greenwood, 1937), p. 9.

2. Harold Bloom makes a similar diagnosis of American theology in *The American Religion* (New York: Simon and Schuster, 1992), arguing that "the essence of the American is the belief that God loves her or him, a conviction shared by nearly nine out of ten of us, according to a Gallup poll. To live in a country where the vast majority so enjoys God's affection is deeply moving, and perhaps an entire society can sustain being the object of so sublime a regard, which after all was granted only to King David in the whole of the Hebrew Bible" (p. 17).

3. Mott, pp. 393–94 (see Ch. 1, n. 3).

4. *Contemplation in a World of Action*, pp. 267–68.

5. Merton, Thomas, *Vow of Conversation: Diary 1964–1965*, ed. Naomi Burton Stone (New York: Farrar, Straus, Giroux, 1988), p. 137.

6. Merton, Thomas, *Faith and Violence: Christian Teaching and Christian Practice* (Notre Dame, Ind.: University of Notre Dame Press, 1968), p. 116.

7. *Conjectures of a Guilty Bystander*, pp. v–vi.

8. *Soul on Ice* (New York: Dell, 1972), p. 44.

9. *Courage for Truth*, p. 84.

10. *New Seeds of Contemplation*, p. 109.

11. Shannon, *Hidden Ground of Love*, p. 294 (see Ch. 4, n. 5).

12. Mott, pp. 435–54.

13. Forest, p. 17 (see Ch. 10, n. 8).

14. Quoted by James Forest in Wilkes, Paul, ed. *Merton by Those Who Knew Him Best* (San Francisco: Harper Row, 1984), p. 55.

15. Merton, Thomas, *The Springs of Contemplation*, ed. Jane Marie Richardson, (New York: Farrar, Straus, Giroux, 1992), pp. 83–84.

16. Rosemary Radford Reuther is the author of many books on religion, politics, and women's spirituality. These include *Gaia and God* (San Francisco: Harper, 1992); *Contemporary Roman Catholicism: Crises and Challenges* (Kansas City, Mo.: Sheed and Ward, 1987); *Sexism and God Talk* (Boston: Beacon, 1987); *Mary: The Feminine Face of the Church* (Philadelphia: Westminster, 1977); and T*he Church Against Itself* (New York: Herder and Herder, 1967).

17. Shannon, *Hidden Ground of Love*, p. 506.

18. *Hidden Ground of Love*, p. 507.

19. *Hidden Ground of Love*, p. 507.

20. Pasternak, Boris, *Doctor Zhivago*, trans. Max Hayward and Manya Harari (New York: Pantheon, 1958), p. 252.

21. This quote comes from an introduction to the correspondence between Merton and Rosemary Ruether recently published under the title *A Home in the World: The Letters of Thomas Merton and Rosemary Ruether*, ed. Mary Tardiff (New York: Orbis, 1995).

22. Letter to author, January 17, 1994.

Chapter Twelve: Zen as Negative Dialectics

1. *Conjectures of a Guilty Bystander*, p. 212.

2. Merton, Thomas, *The Behavior of Titans* (New York: New Directions, 1961), p. 75.

3. *The Behavior of Titans*, p. 83.

4. *The Behavior of Titans*, pp. 83–84.

5. In *Time and Transcendence: Secular History, the Catholic Reaction, and the Recovery of the Future* (Dordrecht/Boston/London: Kluwer, 1992) Gabriel Motzkin contends that "the question is whether Heidegger succeeded in unifying the conceptions of transcendence and time. That was his project, replacing religion not through the denial of the transcendent, nor through the notion that the transcendent can be made immanent, but rather through the idea that the relations between transcendence and time can be defined in such a way as to require no foundation in religion. What then is transcendence if it is neither the world beyond this world, nor the external world? Transcendence here means praxis through which temporality is constituted. That the world is in time is its transcendence. . . . Heidegger's attempt was to take the central experiences of religion, even that of the mystical state of grace, and show not only how one can have them, but how they are necessary for experience, without any reference to any belief whatsoever. In that way, he subverted traditional religion more completely than the secularizers of the preceding centuries. The 'metaphysical', instead of being irrelevant, or belonging to a special domain, turns out to be the concrete" (p. 284–85).

From the point of view of Merton's dialogical theology, Heidegger didn't directly address the religious question; he merely describes the mystery. The religious question is: How are we to respond to it?

6. *The Springs of Contemplation*, pp. 83–84.

7. *The Springs of Contemplation*, pp. 73–74.

8. Merton, Thomas, *The Asian Journal of Thomas Merton*, ed. Naomi Burton, Brother Patrick Hart, and James Laughlin (New York: New Directions, 1973), p. 330.

9. *The Way of Chuang-Tzu* (New York: New Directions, 1965), p. 51.

10. *The Way of Chuang-Tzu*, pp. 52–53.

11. *Faith and Violence: Christian Teaching and Christian Practice*, pp. 145–46.

12. *Conjectures of a Guilty Bystander*, p. 309.

13. Forest, Jim, *Living in Wisdom: A Life of Thomas Merton* (Maryknoll, N.Y.: Orbis Books, 1991), p. 12.

Chapter Thirteen: Journey to the East

1. *The Asian Journal of Thomas Merton*, p. 308.

2. *The Asian Journal of Thomas Merton*, pp. 233, 235.

3. *Conjectures of a Guilty Bystander*, p. 21.

4. *Conjectures of a Guilty Bystander*, p. 129.

Chapter Fourteen: Postmodern Merton?

1. Lacan, Jacques, *Ecrits: A Selection*, trans. Alan Sheridan (New York: Norton, 1977), p. 166.

2. *New Seeds of Contemplation*, pp. 33–34.

3. Merton, Thomas, *Zen and the Birds of Appetite* (New York: New Directions, 1968), pp. 23–24.

4. See for example John Searle, *Minds, Brains and Science* (Cambridge, Mass.: Harvard University Press, 1984) or the groundbreaking work by Jim Culbertson outlined in Nick Herbert's, *Elemental Mind: Human Consciousness and the New Physics* (New York: Dutton, 1993) and further explained in Culberton's forthcoming book, tentatively titled *Physical Psychology*.

5. Merton discusses Brice Parain's influence in his essay "Camus and the Church," in *The Literary Essays of Thomas Merton*, ed. Patrick Hart (New York: New Directions, 1981), pp. 271–72.

6. Merton, Thomas, *The Literary Essays of Thomas Merton*, ed. Brother Patrick Hart (New York: New Directions, 1981), p. 271.

7. *The Literary Essays of Thomas Merton*, p. 275.

8. For a full explication of what it means to speak or to write grammatologically see Gayatri Chakravorty Spivak's translator's preface to *Of Grammatology* by Jacques Derrida (Baltimore: Johns Hopkins University Press, 1976). Derrida remarks: "On what conditions is a grammatology possible? Its fundamental condition is certainly the undoing (solicitation) of logocentrism" (p. 74).

9. *The Literary Essays of Thomas Merton*, p. 276.

10. *Love and Living*, p. 69.

11. *Love and Living*, p. 57.

12. Baudrillard, Jean, *Simulations*, trans. Paul Foss et al. (New York: Semiotext(e), 1983), pp. 42–43.

13. *Disputed Questions*, pp. 179–80.

14. Bloom, Harold, *Ruin the Sacred Truths* (Cambridge, Mass.: Harvard University Press, 1989), p. 5.

15. Merton, Thomas, *Mystics and Zen Masters* (New York: Farrar, Straus, Giroux, 1967), p. 112.

16. *Vow of Conversation*, p. 131.

Conclusion

1. "Informal Talk Delivered at Calcutta, October 1968," quoted in *Thomas Merton: Spiritual Master*, p. 227.

2. *Seven Storey Mountain*, p. 227.

3. *Asian Journal*, p. 68.

4. *Faith and Violence: Christian Teaching and Christian Practice*, p. 213.

5. Fukuyama, Francis, *The End of History and the Last Man* (New York: Free Press, 1992), p. 328.

6. *Conjectures of a Guilty Bystander*, p. 56.

7. Kundera, Milan, *The Art of the Novel* (New York: Grove Press, 1988), p. 20.

8. Merton, Thomas, *The Wisdom of the Desert—Sayings from the Desert Fathers of the Fourth Century*, trans. Thomas Merton (New York: New Directions, 1960), p. 11.

9. *Conjectures of a Guilty Bystander*, p. 64.

10. *Conjectures of a Guilty Bystander*, pp. 154–55.

11. Merton, Thomas, *The Monastic Journey*, ed. Brother Patrick Hart (Garden City, N.Y.: Doubleday, 1978), p. 173.

12. *The Monastic Journey*, p. 61.

13. *The Asian Journal*, p. 13.

INDEX